NOTE TO THE READER

DEDICATION

INTRODUCTION

PART I: FOUNDATIONS OF ORGANIZATIONAL THEORY

CHAPTER 1: HISTORICAL PERSPECTIVES

CHAPTER 2: CORE THEORIES AND CONCEPTS

PART II: ORGANIZATIONAL STRUCTURE AND DESIGN

CHAPTER 3: UNDERSTANDING ORGANIZATIONAL STRUCTURE

CHAPTER 4: DESIGNING EFFECTIVE ORGANIZATIONS

PART III: ORGANIZATIONAL PROCESSES AND DYNAMICS

CHAPTER 5: DECISION-MAKING IN ORGANIZATIONS

CHAPTER 6: POWER, POLITICS, AND INFLUENCE

PART IV: LEADERSHIP AND CULTURE

CHAPTER 7: LEADERSHIP THEORIES AND PRACTICES

8.ORGANIZATIONAL CULTURE AND CLIMATE

PART V: INNOVATION, CHANGE, AND DEVELOPMENT

CHAPTER 9: INNOVATION AND CREATIVITY IN ORGANIZATIONS

10. MANAGING CHANGE AND DEVELOPMENT

PART VI: CONTEMPORARY ISSUES AND FUTURE DIRECTIONS

11. GLOBALIZATION AND ORGANIZATIONAL THEORY

12. FUTURE TRENDS IN ORGANIZATIONAL THEORY

CONCLUSION

Thank you for picking up my book. Your support means a lot, and I hope you find the read both enjoyable and insightful. Beyond being an author, my work extends into research and consultancy within organizational behavior and leadership. I engage with a broad spectrum of clients, from individuals to larger teams and organizations, offering guidance in leadership development.

For a deeper dive into my professional background and consulting philosophy, several websites are available. There, you'll also find my contact details. I'm eager to hear your thoughts on the book or discuss potential collaboration in leadership coaching.

Discover more about my work and other publications related to leadership and organizational behavior at my personal website, https://thomaspatrickhuber.com.

Learn about my specific approach to leadership coaching and consulting at https://elevateus.ch, the official website of my company.

Lastly, in case you want to reach out to me directly please send me an email at thomaspatrick@mac.com.

I appreciate your support in purchasing this book and look forward to connecting with you.

Wishing you an enlightening journey,

Thomas P Huber, PhD, MS ECS

Note to the Reader

This book is based on my more than 30 years of experience as a manager, leader, consultant, and student of organizational theory and application in diverse sectors such as healthcare, banking, and information technology. Throughout my career, I have encountered numerous challenges and opportunities that have shaped my understanding of how organizations function and thrive.

During my PhD work at the University of Berkeley, I had the opportunity to delve deeply into organizational theory. This academic exploration provided many answers to the questions that kept me up at night as a manager. It offered frameworks and insights that illuminated the complexities of organizational life and equipped me with the tools to navigate them more effectively.

My aim with this book is to share these valuable insights and practical strategies with you. Leading modern organizations is no small feat—it is a complex, dynamic, and often daunting task. However, understanding the principles of organizational theory can offer clarity and guidance. This book is designed to help you comprehend the intricacies of organizational structures, cultures, leadership, and change management.

I hope this book will not only deepen your understanding of the complexity of leading modern organizations but also inspire you with the knowledge that there are solutions to the challenges you face. By applying the theories and strategies discussed in these pages, you can drive innovation, foster a positive organizational culture, and navigate change with confidence.

Thank you for embarking on this journey with me. Together, we will explore the rich landscape of organizational theory and discover practical applications that can transform your leadership and your organization.

Dedication

To my mentors, who have been my guiding stars in the vast universe of organizational theory. Your wisdom, patience, and insights have shaped not just my career, but my understanding of what it means to lead and inspire. Thank you for always being there with a piece of advice, a word of encouragement, and the occasional necessary nudge in the right direction.

To my students, you are the spark that ignites my passion for teaching and learning every single day. Your boundless curiosity, tenacity, and innovative spirit make the journey through organizational theory an exciting adventure. Watching you grasp complex concepts and transform them into groundbreaking ideas is a privilege that fills me with immense pride and joy.

To my fellow business people, the men and women who roll up their sleeves and dive into the daily grind with grit and determination. Whether you're leading a multinational corporation, running a startup from your garage, or steering a team through the myriad challenges of modern business, this book is for you. Your stories, your struggles, and your successes have been the heartbeat of this book. May it be a beacon, a source of inspiration, and a practical guide as you navigate the fascinating world of organizational dynamics.

Thank you all for being part of this incredible journey. This book is a tribute to your dedication, your resilience, and your unyielding pursuit of excellence. Let's continue to learn, grow, and succeed together, making our organizations better places to work and thrive. Here's to many more shared successes and transformative moments!

Introduction

Imagine stepping into a bustling office where every employee knows their role, decisions are made with precision, and the organization's culture fosters innovation and satisfaction. Now, envision the opposite: a chaotic environment where miscommunication reigns, resources are wasted, and employee morale is at an all-time low. What separates these two scenarios? The answer lies in understanding and applying the principles of organizational theory.

In "The Structure of Success: Essential Organizational Theories for Business," we demystify the complex world of organizational theory, transforming it into a powerful toolkit for business success. This book is not just about abstract concepts; it's about real-world application and tangible results. Whether you're a CEO, a manager, an entrepreneur, or an aspiring business leader, the insights within these pages will guide you towards creating a high-performing, resilient organization.

From the boardroom to the break room, the principles of organizational theory influence every aspect of a business. Yet, these theories often remain hidden behind academic jargon and complex models. Our mission is to bring these concepts to life, showing you how they apply to everyday business challenges and decisions. Through engaging narratives, relatable examples, and practical advice, we aim to make organizational theory accessible and actionable.

Imagine having the ability to diagnose organizational issues with the precision of a seasoned consultant. Picture leading a team that not only meets but exceeds its goals because you understand the dynamics of power, culture, and innovation. Visualize transforming your organization into a model of efficiency and effectiveness, navigating change with agility and foresight. This book provides the roadmap to achieve these aspirations.

As you turn the pages, you will discover the foundations of organizational theory, learn about the different types of organizational structures, and explore the intricate dynamics of decision-making, power, and leadership. You will gain insights into fostering a positive organizational culture, managing change, and driving innovation. Most importantly, you will see how these theories apply to your own business context, helping you to lead with confidence and clarity.

Join us on this journey as we explore the essential organizational theories that can unlock the potential of your business. The structure of success is within your reach, and it begins with understanding the principles that guide how organizations operate and thrive. Let's dive in and transform the way you think about and lead your organization.

Understanding organizational theory is crucial for business success as it provides a framework for analyzing and improving how organizations function. By studying organizational theory, business professionals can gain insights into the underlying principles that govern organizational behavior, structure, and processes. This knowledge helps in identifying inefficiencies, enhancing communication, and fostering a positive organizational culture.

Organizational theory equips leaders with the tools to make informed decisions about designing organizational structures that align with their strategic objectives. It highlights the importance of adapting to external environments, managing internal dynamics, and leveraging resources effectively. The ability to apply theoretical concepts to practical situations allows businesses to navigate complex challenges and drive continuous improvement. Moreover, organizational theory offers a lens through which to view the impact of leadership, power, and politics within an organization. Understanding these dynamics enables leaders to foster collaboration, resolve conflicts, and build cohesive teams. It also sheds light on the role of organizational culture in shaping employee behavior and organizational outcomes.

In a rapidly changing business landscape, the principles of organizational theory are more relevant than ever. They provide a foundation for understanding how organizations can innovate, adapt, and thrive amidst uncertainty. By integrating these theories into their practice, business professionals can develop strategies that not only enhance performance but also ensure long-term sustainability.

Organizational theory is not just an academic exercise; it is a practical toolkit that can transform the way businesses operate. It helps leaders see the bigger picture, anticipate challenges, and implement solutions that drive success. As we jump into the various theories and their applications, we will uncover the ways in which organizational theory can be a powerful catalyst for business excellence.

Purpose of the Book

"The Structure of Success: Essential Organizational Theories for Business" aims to bridge the gap between complex organizational theories and the practical needs of business professionals. This book is designed to be an engaging, accessible guide that demystifies organizational theory and demonstrates its relevance through real-world examples and practical applications.

Why This Book?

- Make Theory Practical: Organizational theories can often seem abstract and disconnected from everyday business operations. This book transforms these theories into practical tools that business professionals can use to enhance their organizational effectiveness.

- Engage and Inspire: Using a dialogue-driven narrative, the book seeks to engage readers by presenting theories through relatable stories, case studies, and hypothetical scenarios. This approach ensures that concepts are not only understood but also retained and applied.

- Comprehensive Overview: Covering a broad spectrum of organizational theories, from foundational ideas to contemporary issues, the book provides a comprehensive overview that equips readers with a well-rounded understanding of the field.

- Actionable Insights: Each chapter concludes with key takeaways and actionable insights that readers can implement in their own organizations. This practical focus ensures that the book serves as a valuable resource for immediate application.

- Relatable Examples: By incorporating examples from various industries and organizational contexts, the book illustrates how organizational theories apply across different business environments, making it relevant to a wide audience.

Who Should Read This Book?

- Executives and Managers: Gain insights into how organizational structures and processes can be optimized to achieve strategic goals.

- Entrepreneurs and Start-Up Founders: Learn how to build robust organizational frameworks that support growth and innovation.

- Students and Academics: Explore practical applications of organizational theories that complement academic studies.

- Business Consultants and Advisors: Enhance your toolkit with proven strategies and insights to guide your clients effectively.

We are committed to making this journey through organizational theory as engaging and valuable as possible. Through a blend of narration, dialogue, and real-life examples, we aim to bring the world of organizations to life, showing how these concepts can drive success in any business setting. Join us as we explore the intricacies of organizational dynamics and unlock the secrets to building high-performing, resilient organizations.

Organizational theory encompasses a wide array of concepts that help explain how organizations operate and succeed. At its core, the theory examines the formal and informal structures within an organization, the roles and relationships among its members, and the external environment that influences its functioning.

One of the foundational concepts in organizational theory is the distinction between different types of systems. Closed systems view organizations as self-contained entities that are largely unaffected by their external environment. In contrast, open systems recognize that organizations interact continuously with their external environment, requiring them to adapt and respond to external changes to survive and thrive. This open systems perspective has become increasingly important in today's dynamic business landscape.

Rationality in decision-making is another key concept. Traditional theories often assumed that individuals within organizations act rationally, making decisions that maximize efficiency and effectiveness. However, Herbert Simon introduced the idea of bounded rationality, acknowledging that individuals operate under constraints that limit their ability to make fully rational decisions. Instead, they often settle for "satisficing" – seeking solutions that are good enough rather than optimal.

Power and politics are integral to understanding organizational behavior. Power dynamics influence decision-making processes, resource allocation, and the relationships between different organizational members and units. Recognizing how power operates within an organization can help leaders navigate internal politics and build more effective strategies for achieving their goals.

Leadership and organizational culture are also central themes. Effective leadership is critical for guiding organizations through change, fostering innovation, and maintaining a motivated workforce. Organizational culture, defined by shared values, beliefs, and norms, shapes how members of the organization interact and work together. A strong, positive culture can enhance performance and employee satisfaction, while a toxic culture can lead to dysfunction and high turnover.

Innovation and change management are crucial for organizational resilience. Organizations must continually innovate to stay competitive and adapt to changing market conditions. Theories of innovation explore how new ideas are generated, developed, and implemented within organizations. Change management focuses on the strategies and processes that help organizations transition smoothly through periods of change, minimizing disruption and maximizing the benefits of new initiatives.

Contemporary issues such as globalization, technological advancements, and sustainability are increasingly important in organizational theory. Globalization expands the competitive landscape and introduces new cultural dynamics that organizations must navigate. Technological advancements, including artificial intelligence and digital transformation, are reshaping how organizations operate. Sustainability and ethical practices are becoming central to organizational strategy, as businesses recognize their responsibility to society and the environment.

Understanding these key concepts provides a comprehensive foundation for analyzing and improving organizational effectiveness. As we explore each of these areas in more detail, we will illustrate their practical applications through real-world examples and case studies, making the theory accessible and relevant to everyday business practice.

Part I: Foundations of Organizational Theory

To navigate the complexities of modern business, it's essential to understand the fundamental principles that underpin organizational behavior and structure. Part I of this book, "Foundations of Organizational Theory," takes you on a journey through the origins and evolution of the ideas that have shaped our understanding of organizations today.

The early pioneers of organizational theory, such as Frederick Taylor, Henri Fayol, and Max Weber, laid the groundwork with their groundbreaking ideas on management and structure. Their contributions, while sometimes viewed as rigid or overly mechanistic, provided the first systematic approaches to improving organizational efficiency and effectiveness. Taylor's scientific management, Fayol's administrative principles, and Weber's bureaucracy each offered unique insights into how organizations could be structured and managed to achieve their goals.

As businesses and industries evolved, so too did the recognition that organizations are not merely machines but are composed of complex human relationships. The Human Relations Movement emerged in response to this understanding, emphasizing the importance of social and psychological factors in the workplace. This shift highlighted the need for managers to consider employee morale, motivation, and group dynamics, moving beyond the purely technical aspects of work.

Building on these early theories, modern organizational thought has expanded to include a range of perspectives that address the dynamic and multifaceted nature of organizations. Contingency theory, for example, suggests that there is no one-size-fits-all solution to organizational design; instead, the best structure depends on various internal and external factors. Systems theory further enriches our understanding by viewing organizations as open systems that constantly interact with their environments, emphasizing the importance of adaptability and holistic thinking.

In the chapters that follow, we will dig into the core concepts and theories that form the backbone of organizational theory. You will explore different ways of viewing organizations—as rational systems focused on efficiency, as natural systems centered on human and social aspects, and as open systems that interact with and adapt to their environments. Key theories such as bounded rationality, sensemaking, resource dependency, and institutional theory will provide deeper insights into decision-making processes, power dynamics, and the role of legitimacy in organizational success.

By understanding these foundational perspectives, you will be equipped with the knowledge to analyze and improve your own organization. Whether you are a manager looking to enhance your leadership skills, a business owner striving to create a more effective organization, or a student eager to grasp the complexities of organizational behavior, this part of the book will provide you with the essential building blocks to achieve your goals. Remember that these ideas are not just academic concepts. They are practical tools that, when applied thoughtfully, can transform the way you lead, manage, and navigate the challenges of today's business world. Welcome to the foundations of organizational theory—a journey that will illuminate the structures and processes that drive organizational success.

Chapter 1: Historical Perspectives

To truly grasp the intricacies of modern organizational theory, we must first look back at its roots. Chapter 1, "Historical Perspectives," sets the stage by examining the seminal theories and movements that have shaped the field. Understanding these foundational ideas provides the necessary context to appreciate how far organizational theory has come and the directions it may take in the future.

Our journey begins with the early pioneers: Frederick Winslow Taylor, Henri Fayol, and Max Weber. Each of these thinkers introduced groundbreaking concepts that revolutionized the way organizations were structured and managed.

Taylorism, or scientific management, introduced by Frederick Winslow Taylor in the early 20th century, emphasized efficiency and productivity through systematic observation and measurement of work processes. Taylor's principles sought to optimize labor by breaking down tasks into their simplest components, establishing standard procedures, and training workers to perform tasks in the most efficient manner possible. His ideas were a significant departure from the more ad-hoc management practices of his time and laid the groundwork for modern operational efficiency.

Meanwhile, Henri Fayol, a contemporary of Taylor, focused on the broader aspects of management with his administrative theory. Fayol identified key managerial functions—planning, organizing, commanding, coordinating, and controlling—that he believed were essential for organizational success. His 14 principles of management, which include concepts such as division of work, authority and responsibility, and unity of command, provided a comprehensive framework for effective management practices that are still taught and applied today.

Max Weber, a German sociologist, introduced the concept of bureaucracy as an ideal type of organizational structure. Weber's model emphasized a clear hierarchy, division of labor, and a set of formal rules and procedures designed to ensure efficiency, predictability, and rationality in organizational operations. While Weber's bureaucracy has been critiqued for its potential rigidity, it remains a fundamental concept in understanding organizational structure and governance.

As the industrial era progressed, the limitations of these mechanistic approaches became apparent. Workers were not merely cogs in a machine; they were human beings with social and psychological needs. This realization gave rise to the Human Relations Movement, spearheaded by researchers like Elton Mayo. The famous Hawthorne Studies conducted by Mayo and his colleagues highlighted the importance of social relations and employee well-being in the workplace. These studies demonstrated that factors such as attention from supervisors, a sense of belonging, and supportive work environments could significantly enhance worker productivity and satisfaction.

The evolution of organizational theory did not stop there. The latter half of the 20th century and beyond saw the emergence of modern developments that integrated and expanded upon earlier ideas. The contingency theory introduced the notion that there is no one best way to organize; instead, the optimal structure depends on various internal and external factors. Systems theory provided a holistic view of organizations as open systems interacting with their environments, emphasizing adaptability and interdependence. These and other modern theories have enriched our understanding of organizational dynamics, making them more relevant to the complexities of today's business environment.

We will explore these historical perspectives, examining the contributions of Taylor, Fayol, and Weber, exploring the impact of the Human Relations Movement, and tracing the evolution of modern organizational theory. By understanding where these ideas originated and how they developed, we can better appreciate their application and relevance in contemporary organizational contexts.

The foundations of organizational theory were laid by three pioneering thinkers whose work continues to influence modern management practices: Frederick Winslow Taylor, Henri Fayol, and Max Weber. Each of these theorists offered distinct perspectives on how organizations should be structured and managed to achieve maximum efficiency and effectiveness.

Taylorism (Scientific Management)

Frederick Winslow Taylor, often referred to as the father of scientific management, introduced a methodical approach to improving labor productivity. His theory, known as Taylorism, was developed in the early 20th century and focused on the optimization of work processes through scientific analysis. Taylor believed that by studying tasks and workflows scientifically, managers could identify the most efficient ways to perform jobs.

Taylor's principles of scientific management included:

- Time and Motion Studies: By analyzing the time and movements required to perform tasks, Taylor sought to eliminate unnecessary actions and streamline workflows.

- Standardization: Establishing standard procedures and tools for tasks to ensure consistency and efficiency.

- Specialization: Breaking down tasks into simple, repetitive components and assigning them to workers best suited for each task.

- Training: Providing workers with specific instructions and training to perform tasks in the prescribed manner.

- Incentive Systems: Implementing performance-based pay to motivate workers to achieve higher productivity.

Taylor's approach was revolutionary in its emphasis on efficiency and productivity, transforming industrial operations and laying the groundwork for modern operational management. However, critics argued that Taylorism dehumanized workers by treating them as mere parts of a machine, neglecting their social and psychological needs.

Fayol's Administrative Theory

Henri Fayol, a contemporary of Taylor, offered a broader perspective on management that extended beyond the shop floor to encompass the entire organization. Fayol's administrative theory, articulated in his 1916 book "General and Industrial Management," identified key functions and principles of management that he believed were essential for organizational success.

Fayol's five functions of management were:

- Planning: Developing a plan of action to achieve organizational goals.

- Organizing: Arranging resources and tasks to implement the plan.

- Commanding: Leading and directing employees to carry out tasks.

- Coordinating: Ensuring that all parts of the organization work together harmoniously.

- Controlling: Monitoring performance and making necessary adjustments to stay on track.

In addition to these functions, Fayol proposed 14 principles of management, including:

- Division of Work: Specializing tasks to increase efficiency.

- Authority and Responsibility: Ensuring that managers have the authority to give orders and the responsibility to achieve results.

- Discipline: Maintaining respect and compliance within the organization.

- Unity of Command: Each employee should receive orders from only one superior.

- Unity of Direction: All activities should be aligned towards the same objectives.

- Scalar Chain: Establishing a clear line of authority from top management to the lowest ranks.

Fayol's holistic approach to management provided a comprehensive framework that extended beyond operational efficiency to include strategic and administrative considerations. His work remains influential in contemporary management education and practice.

Weber's Bureaucratic Theory

Max Weber, a German sociologist, introduced the concept of bureaucracy as an ideal organizational structure. Weber's bureaucratic theory, developed in the early 20th century, was based on the idea that organizations could achieve efficiency and predictability through a formalized and rational structure.

Key features of Weber's bureaucracy included:

- Hierarchical Structure: A clear chain of command with each level of authority reporting to a higher level.

- Division of Labor: Specialized roles and responsibilities for each position to ensure expertise and efficiency.

- Formal Rules and Procedures: Written policies and procedures to govern all organizational activities, ensuring consistency and fairness.

- Impersonal Relationships: Decisions and interactions based on rules and roles rather than personal relationships, reducing favoritism and bias.

- Merit-Based Advancement: Employment and promotion based on qualifications and performance rather than personal connections.

Weber believed that bureaucracy was the most rational and efficient way to organize large, complex organizations. While his model aimed to eliminate the arbitrariness and inefficiency of traditional management practices, it also faced criticism for being overly rigid and dehumanizing.

Together, the contributions of Taylor, Fayol, and Weber provided the foundational theories that have shaped modern organizational management. Their insights into efficiency, administrative functions, and formal structures continue to inform contemporary practices, even as organizations adapt to new challenges and environments. Understanding these early theories is crucial for appreciating the evolution and application of organizational theory in today's dynamic business landscape.

Modern Developments in Organizational Theory

As organizations have evolved in response to technological advancements, globalization, and changing societal values, so too has the field of organizational theory. Modern developments in this area build on the foundational theories of the past while addressing the complexities and dynamic nature of contemporary business environments. This chapter explores several key modern theories that have significantly influenced organizational thought and practice.

Contingency Theory

One of the significant developments in organizational theory is contingency theory, which emerged in the 1960s. Unlike earlier theories that sought universal principles applicable to all organizations, contingency theory posits that there is no one best way to organize. Instead, the optimal organizational structure and management practices depend on various internal and external factors.

Key concepts of contingency theory include:

- Fit and Adaptation: Organizations must adapt their structures and processes to fit their specific environments. Factors such as size, technology, environment, and strategy influence the most appropriate organizational design.

- Environmental Uncertainty: Organizations operate in environments that vary in terms of complexity and uncertainty. Those facing high uncertainty need more flexible and adaptive structures, while those in stable environments can benefit from more formalized and rigid structures.

- Differentiation and Integration: Different organizational units may require different structures and processes depending on their tasks and goals. Effective organizations balance the need for differentiation (specialized units) with integration (coordination among units).

Systems Theory

Systems theory views organizations as open systems that interact with their environments. This perspective emphasizes the interconnectedness and interdependence of various organizational elements, including people, processes, and technology.

Key elements of systems theory include:

- Holistic View: Organizations are seen as whole systems composed of interrelated parts. Changes in one part of the system can affect the entire organization.

- Inputs, Throughputs, and Outputs: Organizations receive inputs (resources, information) from their environment, transform these inputs through various processes, and produce outputs (products, services) that are delivered back to the environment.

- Feedback Loops: Organizations rely on feedback from their environment to adjust and improve their processes. Feedback mechanisms help organizations learn and adapt to changes.

Resource Dependency Theory

Developed by Jeffrey Pfeffer and Gerald Salancik in the late 1970s, resource dependency theory focuses on how organizations manage external dependencies to secure essential resources. The theory highlights the power dynamics and strategic behaviors organizations employ to manage their relationships with external entities.

Key aspects of resource dependency theory include:

- Resource Control: Organizations depend on external resources such as raw materials, information, and financial capital. Controlling these resources can create power imbalances and dependencies.

- Strategic Alliances and Partnerships: To reduce dependency and uncertainty, organizations form alliances, joint ventures, and partnerships. These strategies help organizations secure critical resources and gain a competitive advantage.

- Environmental Scanning: Organizations continuously monitor their environments to identify and respond to changes that may affect resource availability and stability.

Institutional Theory

Institutional theory, articulated by scholars such as John Meyer and Brian Rowan, examines how organizations conform to societal norms, values, and expectations to gain legitimacy and ensure survival. The theory suggests that organizations are influenced by cultural, normative, and regulatory pressures from their institutional environments.

Key concepts of institutional theory include:

- Isomorphism: Organizations tend to become similar to each other over time as they adopt similar structures and practices to gain legitimacy. This process is driven by coercive (regulatory), mimetic (imitative), and normative (professional) isomorphism.

- Legitimacy: Organizations seek legitimacy by aligning with accepted norms and practices within their institutional environments. Legitimacy enhances an organization's credibility and support from stakeholders.

- Decoupling: Sometimes, organizations adopt formal structures and practices to appear legitimate while actual operations remain unchanged. This phenomenon is known as decoupling, where the symbolic adoption of practices does not translate into substantive change.

Sensemaking in Organizations

Karl Weick's sensemaking theory focuses on how individuals and organizations interpret and give meaning to their experiences. Sensemaking is a continuous process that involves constructing and reconstructing understanding through actions and interactions.

Key elements of sensemaking include:

- Retrospective Interpretation: People make sense of events by reflecting on past experiences and actions. This retrospective process helps them understand and navigate current situations.

- Social Process: Sensemaking is inherently social, involving communication and interaction with others. Shared meanings and interpretations emerge through collective sensemaking.

- Enactment: Individuals and organizations create their environments through their actions. These enacted environments, in turn, shape their perceptions and understandings.

Complexity Theory and Adaptive Systems

Complexity theory views organizations as complex adaptive systems that evolve in unpredictable and nonlinear ways. This perspective emphasizes the importance of flexibility, innovation, and responsiveness in dynamic and uncertain environments.

Key concepts of complexity theory include:

- Emergence: Complex systems exhibit emergent properties that arise from the interactions of their components. These properties are often unpredictable and cannot be understood by examining individual parts in isolation.

- Self-Organization: Complex systems can self-organize without central control. Organizational structures and patterns emerge spontaneously through interactions among individuals and groups.

- Adaptation: Organizations must continuously adapt to changing conditions. This adaptive capability is essential for survival and success in turbulent environments.

These modern developments in organizational theory provide valuable insights and frameworks for understanding and managing contemporary organizations. They highlight the importance of adaptability, strategic resource management, institutional alignment, and continuous sensemaking in navigating the complexities of today's business world.

By integrating these theories into their practice, managers and leaders can develop more resilient, innovative, and responsive organizations. The insights from contingency theory, systems theory, resource dependency, institutional theory, sensemaking, and complexity theory offer practical tools and strategies for addressing the challenges and opportunities of the modern business environment.

As we explore these modern developments, we will illustrate their application through real-world examples and case studies, demonstrating how these theories can drive organizational success and transformation. Understanding and leveraging these modern theories is essential for building organizations that are not only efficient and effective but also adaptive and resilient in the face of change.

Contingency theory is significant because it teaches us that there is no single best way to manage an organization. Successful management depends on understanding the specific context and adapting accordingly. For today's managers, this means customizing strategies and structures to fit their organization's unique environment, size, and goals. It involves continuously monitoring external conditions such as market trends, technological advancements, and regulatory changes, and adjusting strategies proactively. In a world where change is constant, being agile and adaptable is crucial. Contingency theory equips managers with the mindset to embrace change rather than resist it.

Systems theory emphasizes the interconnectedness of various organizational elements and their interaction with the external environment. For modern managers, this holistic view is vital because it fosters an awareness of interdependency. Understanding that changes in one part of the organization can affect other parts helps managers make more informed and strategic decisions. By viewing the organization as a system of inputs, throughputs, and outputs, managers can optimize processes to enhance efficiency and effectiveness. Recognizing the organization's role within a broader ecosystem encourages sustainable practices and long-term thinking.

Resource dependency theory highlights the importance of managing external dependencies to secure essential resources. Managers today must build strategic alliances to help organizations secure critical resources and reduce dependency on any single source. Developing skills in negotiation and influence is essential to managing relationships with suppliers, customers, regulators, and other stakeholders. By understanding their resource dependencies, managers can identify potential vulnerabilities and develop strategies to mitigate risks.

Institutional theory underscores the importance of aligning with societal norms, values, and expectations to gain legitimacy. For contemporary managers, this means aligning organizational practices with societal expectations to build a positive brand reputation and trust among stakeholders. Adhering to regulatory requirements and industry standards ensures that the organization avoids legal issues and maintains operational integrity. Developing an organizational culture that reflects broader societal values attracts top talent and fosters employee loyalty.

Karl Weick's sensemaking theory focuses on interpreting and making sense of complex and ambiguous situations. Managers can benefit from this by facilitating clear and continuous communication to ensure that team members have a shared understanding of goals and challenges. Being able to reinterpret and adjust strategies based on new information and changing circumstances is critical in today's fast-paced environment. Leaders who can help their teams make sense of their roles and the organization's direction can foster greater engagement and commitment.

Complexity theory views organizations as complex adaptive systems. For managers, this perspective is crucial for fostering innovation and resilience because it encourages embracing uncertainty. Accepting that uncertainty and unpredictability are inherent in complex systems fosters a culture of experimentation and innovation. Encouraging self-organization and decentralized decision-making can lead to more innovative solutions and faster responses to change. Understanding how to build systems that can adapt and thrive amidst disruption ensures that the organization remains robust and competitive.

These modern theories provide actionable insights that managers can apply in various practical scenarios. For strategic planning, managers can use contingency and systems theories to develop flexible and integrated strategic plans. Applying sensemaking and complexity theories can guide organizations through transformational change. Leveraging resource dependency theory can optimize the allocation of critical resources. Utilizing institutional theory ensures that organizational practices align with ethical standards and regulatory requirements. Encouraging a culture of innovation by applying complexity theory principles, such as fostering experimentation and embracing failure as a learning opportunity, can drive organizational success.

The relevance of these modern organizational theories lies in their ability to provide managers with the frameworks and tools needed to address the challenges of today's dynamic business environment. By integrating these theories into their daily practice, managers can enhance their decision-making, foster a positive organizational culture, drive innovation, and ensure long-term sustainability and success. Understanding and applying these theories is not just an academic exercise; it's a strategic imperative for any manager aiming to lead a high-performing and resilient organization in the modern world.

As we explore the complexities of modern organizational theories, we will bring these concepts to life through a series of hypothetical case examples. These scenarios are designed to illustrate how the theories can be practically applied to address real-world challenges. By understanding and leveraging these theories, managers can create more adaptable, resilient, and effective organizations. You will encounter examples like AlphaTech, a manufacturing company adapting its structure to fit a dynamic market environment, and GreenWave, a nonprofit organization maximizing its impact through integrated efforts. You'll see how BetaHealth diversifies its funding sources to reduce dependency, and how EcoMarket aligns its practices with societal values to enhance legitimacy. FutureTech's journey of making sense of internal challenges and Gamma Innovations' embrace of complexity theory to foster innovation will also provide valuable insights.

These examples will help you visualize the application of theories such as contingency theory, systems theory, resource dependency theory, institutional theory, sensemaking, and complexity theory. By seeing these concepts in action, you will gain a deeper understanding of how to apply them within your own organization to navigate challenges and drive success. Let's dive into these fascinating stories and uncover the practical wisdom they offer for today's managers.

Contingency Theory

Imagine a mid-sized manufacturing company, AlphaTech, facing increased competition from overseas firms. The company has always followed a rigid hierarchical structure with centralized decision-making. However, market conditions are changing rapidly, and customer demands are becoming more diverse. To stay competitive, AlphaTech's CEO decides to apply contingency theory. She restructures the organization into semi-autonomous units, each focusing on different product lines. This new structure allows each unit to respond more quickly to market changes and customer needs. For instance, the unit responsible for high-tech gadgets can innovate faster without waiting for approvals from the central office. By adapting the organizational structure to fit the specific market environment, AlphaTech successfully navigates the competitive landscape.

Systems Theory

GreenWave, a nonprofit organization focused on environmental sustainability, operates various projects ranging from clean energy initiatives to wildlife conservation. The executive director notices that while each project is successful on its own, there is little synergy between them, leading to missed opportunities for greater impact. Applying systems theory, the director reimagines GreenWave as an interconnected system. She establishes cross-functional teams that include members from different projects to work on joint initiatives. For example, a team might combine efforts from the clean energy and conservation projects to create a solar-powered wildlife sanctuary. By fostering interconnectedness and integrating efforts, GreenWave maximizes its resources and amplifies its impact on environmental sustainability.

Resource Dependency Theory

BetaHealth, a healthcare provider, relies heavily on government funding for its operations. Recently, policy changes have threatened this funding, putting BetaHealth's financial stability at risk. The management team realizes they need to diversify their funding sources to reduce dependency. Using resource dependency theory, BetaHealth's leaders develop strategies to form alliances with private investors and philanthropic organizations. They launch community health programs funded by grants and partner with local businesses to offer employee wellness services. By broadening their resource base, BetaHealth reduces its vulnerability to government policy changes and secures a more stable financial future.

Institutional Theory

EcoMarket, a retail company specializing in eco-friendly products, wants to strengthen its brand reputation and align more closely with societal values. The company decides to pursue certification as a B Corporation, which requires meeting high standards of social and environmental performance, accountability, and transparency. By adopting institutional theory, EcoMarket undergoes changes to comply with the certification requirements. This includes implementing fair labor practices, reducing carbon footprints, and increasing transparency in supply chain operations. These changes not only enhance EcoMarket's legitimacy and appeal to socially conscious consumers but also attract top talent who are passionate about sustainability.

Sensemaking in Organizations

FutureTech, a fast-growing tech startup, experiences a sudden drop in employee morale and productivity after a rapid expansion. The leadership team is puzzled and needs to understand what went wrong. They decide to engage in sensemaking to diagnose the issue. The CEO initiates a series of town hall meetings and small group discussions, encouraging employees to share their experiences and concerns. Through these interactions, the leadership team learns that employees feel disconnected and overwhelmed by the rapid changes. In response, FutureTech implements a mentorship program, improves internal communication channels, and creates opportunities for team bonding. By making sense of the employees' experiences and addressing their concerns, FutureTech rebuilds its positive work culture and restores productivity.

Complexity Theory

Gamma Innovations, a technology firm, operates in a highly volatile market where rapid innovation is crucial for survival. The company's traditional hierarchical structure slows down decision-making and stifles creativity. Applying complexity theory, Gamma Innovations embraces a more flexible and decentralized structure. They create small, self-organizing teams empowered to make decisions and experiment with new ideas. For instance, a team working on a new software product is given the autonomy to pivot and iterate based on market feedback without seeking higher approval for each change. This approach fosters innovation and allows the company to adapt quickly to market shifts, keeping it at the forefront of the tech industry.

Chapter 2: Core Theories and Concepts

We invite you now to the core theories and concepts that provide a deep understanding of how organizations operate. These theories offer valuable insights into the various dimensions of organizational life, from the formal structures and rational processes to the informal social dynamics and environmental interactions. By exploring these foundational perspectives, we equip managers with the tools they need to navigate the complexities of modern organizational environments effectively.

Organizations can be viewed through different lenses, each offering unique insights into their functioning. The rational systems perspective emphasizes formal structures and efficiency, treating organizations like well-oiled machines designed to achieve specific goals. The natural systems perspective focuses on the social aspects, recognizing that organizations are composed of individuals with their own needs and interactions. The open systems perspective extends these views by considering the continuous exchange between the organization and its external environment, highlighting adaptability and responsiveness.

Herbert Simon introduced the concept of bounded rationality, challenging the notion that individuals make perfectly rational decisions. Instead, decision-makers operate under constraints such as limited information, time, and cognitive capacity. Simon's idea of satisficing suggests that individuals seek solutions that are "good enough" rather than optimal, acknowledging the practical limitations they face in real-world decision-making.

Karl Weick's sensemaking theory emphasizes the process by which individuals and organizations interpret and give meaning to their experiences. Sensemaking involves constructing and reconstructing understanding through actions and interactions.

This perspective highlights the fluid and ongoing nature of organizational life and the importance of context and perception in shaping organizational behavior.

Jeffrey Pfeffer and Gerald Salancik's resource dependency theory focuses on how organizations manage their dependencies on external resources. The theory posits that organizations are influenced by the power dynamics created by these dependencies. Managing relationships with suppliers, customers, and other stakeholders becomes crucial for securing essential resources and maintaining stability.

Institutional theory, articulated by scholars like John Meyer and Brian Rowan, explores how organizations conform to societal norms, values, and expectations to gain legitimacy. This theory suggests that organizations adopt formal structures and practices not just for efficiency but to align with institutionalized rules and gain social acceptance. It underscores the role of culture, norms, and legitimacy in shaping organizational behavior.

In today's fast-paced and complex business environment, these theories provide critical insights that help managers make informed decisions, foster a positive organizational culture, and navigate change effectively. Understanding the interplay between formal structures, social dynamics, and environmental interactions enables managers to create more adaptable, resilient, and effective organizations.

Understanding organizations requires looking at them through different lenses. The three primary perspectives—rational, natural, and open systems—each offer unique insights into how organizations function and succeed.

Rational Systems

The rational systems perspective views organizations as formal structures designed to achieve specific goals efficiently. This approach emphasizes logical, planned, and systematic procedures, focusing on clear objectives, defined roles, and established rules.

In rational systems, the organization is akin to a machine, where each part has a specific function, and the overall system is designed for optimal performance. Managers within this framework prioritize precision, predictability, and control. This perspective is foundational in many traditional management theories, including Taylorism and Weber's bureaucracy, which advocate for structured, rule-based operations to maximize efficiency and productivity.

Consider a manufacturing company that implements a highly regimented production process. Every task is carefully timed and standardized to ensure maximum efficiency. Employees are trained to perform specific roles, and strict protocols are followed to maintain quality and minimize waste. In this rational system, the focus is on achieving the organization's goals with precision and consistency.

Natural Systems

In contrast to the rational perspective, the natural systems approach views organizations as social systems, emphasizing the importance of human behavior, social relationships, and informal structures. This perspective acknowledges that organizations are composed of individuals with their own needs, motivations, and interactions, which can significantly impact organizational outcomes.

Natural systems theory highlights the importance of culture, values, and the informal networks that develop within organizations. It suggests that while formal structures and rules are important, much of what happens within an organization is driven by informal social processes and human interactions.

Imagine a tech startup where creativity and innovation are paramount. The formal organizational chart may show specific roles and reporting lines, but much of the company's success comes from the informal interactions and collaborations among employees. Team members frequently engage in spontaneous brainstorming sessions, and decisions are often influenced by the shared values and culture of the organization. This natural system thrives on flexibility, employee engagement, and a strong sense of community.

Open Systems

The open systems perspective integrates both the rational and natural approaches but extends beyond them by considering the organization's interaction with its external environment. Open systems theory posits that organizations are not isolated entities; they constantly exchange information, resources, and influences with their surroundings.

This perspective emphasizes the importance of adaptability, responsiveness, and sustainability. Organizations must be able to adjust to environmental changes, such as market dynamics, technological advancements, and regulatory shifts, to survive and thrive. Open systems are characterized by continuous feedback loops, where information from the environment informs organizational processes and decisions, leading to ongoing adaptation and learning.

Consider an international retail company that operates in diverse markets around the world. To succeed, it must continually monitor external factors such as consumer preferences, economic conditions, and competitive actions. The company adapts its strategies based on this feedback, whether by introducing new product lines, modifying marketing approaches, or adjusting supply chain operations. This open system is dynamic and responsive, ensuring that the organization remains relevant and competitive in a changing environment.

Application of Systems Perspectives

These three systems perspectives provide a comprehensive framework for understanding different aspects of organizational life. The rational perspective focuses on structure and efficiency, the natural perspective emphasizes social dynamics and culture, and the open perspective highlights the importance of environmental interactions and adaptability.

Managers can apply these perspectives to diagnose organizational issues, develop strategies, and implement changes. For instance, a manager might use the rational perspective to streamline operations and improve efficiency, the natural perspective to enhance employee engagement and foster a positive culture, and the open perspective to adapt to market changes and ensure long-term sustainability.

By integrating these perspectives, managers can develop a more holistic understanding of their organizations, leading to more effective and balanced decision-making. The interplay between formal structures, social dynamics, and environmental interactions is crucial for achieving organizational success in today's complex and dynamic business landscape.

In the following sections, we will explore additional core theories and concepts that build on these foundational perspectives, providing deeper insights into organizational behavior and management practices.

Herbert Simon's groundbreaking work on bounded rationality and satisficing offers a profound shift from the classical view of rational decision-making. Traditional economic and management theories often assume that individuals make perfectly rational decisions, optimizing outcomes by weighing all possible alternatives and selecting the best option. However, Simon recognized that real-world decision-making is rarely this idealized due to inherent human limitations.

Bounded Rationality

Bounded rationality acknowledges that individuals operate under constraints that limit their ability to process information and make optimal decisions. These constraints include limited time, incomplete information, and cognitive limitations. Simon argued that rather than being fully rational, individuals are "boundedly rational," meaning their rationality is constrained by these limitations.

In the context of bounded rationality, decision-makers use heuristics—simplified rules or strategies—to make decisions. These heuristics help manage complexity and uncertainty but can also lead to biases and errors. By understanding the concept of bounded rationality, managers can better appreciate the challenges their teams face in decision-making processes and can design systems that account for these human limitations.

Satisficing

Given the constraints of bounded rationality, Simon introduced the concept of satisficing as an alternative to the notion of optimization. Satisficing involves seeking a solution that is "good enough" rather than the best possible one. Decision-makers aim to meet acceptable criteria rather than achieve the optimal outcome, which is often impractical or impossible given their constraints.

Satisficing is a pragmatic approach that balances the need for a satisfactory solution with the realities of limited resources and information. It allows organizations to make timely decisions without getting paralyzed by the quest for perfection.

Practical Application of Bounded Rationality and Satisficing

Let's consider a hypothetical case of a mid-sized healthcare provider, BetaHealth, deciding to implement a new electronic health record (EHR) system. The management team faces several constraints: they have limited time to make a decision, incomplete information about all available EHR systems, and varying opinions among stakeholders about the best features and functionalities.

Recognizing these limitations, the team adopts a satisficing approach. Instead of trying to find the perfect EHR system, they define a set of essential criteria that the new system must meet, such as compatibility with existing infrastructure, user-friendliness, and compliance with healthcare regulations. After evaluating several options, they select a system that meets these criteria adequately, even if it is not the optimal choice in every aspect.

By satisficing, BetaHealth can move forward with the implementation without excessive delays, ensuring that they have a functional and acceptable solution in place. This approach allows them to adapt and make further adjustments as needed, rather than being stuck in the decision-making process.

Understanding bounded rationality and satisficing is crucial for today's managers for several reasons:

- Realistic Expectations: Managers can set realistic expectations for themselves and their teams by acknowledging the limitations of human decision-making. This understanding fosters a more supportive and realistic approach to problem-solving.

- Efficient Decision-Making: By adopting satisficing strategies, managers can make timely decisions that meet necessary criteria without being bogged down by the pursuit of perfection. This is particularly important in fast-paced environments where delays can be costly.

- Designing Better Systems: Managers can design decision-making processes and systems that account for bounded rationality. For example, they can provide clear criteria for decisions, simplify information processing, and offer decision support tools to help employees navigate complex choices.

- Reducing Cognitive Load: Understanding that employees have cognitive limitations can lead managers to create work environments that reduce unnecessary cognitive load. This might include minimizing multitasking, providing adequate resources, and encouraging breaks to enhance focus and productivity.

- Encouraging Flexibility: By promoting a satisficing approach, managers encourage flexibility and adaptability. Employees are empowered to make decisions that are good enough to move forward, knowing that they can adjust and improve as they learn more.

Herbert Simon's concepts of bounded rationality and satisficing offer invaluable insights into the realities of decision-making within organizations. By embracing these ideas, managers can create more effective, realistic, and supportive environments that enable better decision-making and ultimately drive organizational success. As we continue exploring core theories and concepts, keep these principles in mind and consider how they can be applied to enhance your management practices.

Karl Weick's theory of sensemaking offers a powerful lens through which to understand how individuals and organizations interpret and navigate complex and ambiguous situations. Sensemaking is not just about understanding the world; it is about constructing reality through interactions and actions. Weick's perspective emphasizes the dynamic and iterative process by which meaning is created, making it particularly relevant for organizations operating in volatile and uncertain environments.

Sensemaking involves several key elements that distinguish it from other cognitive processes:

1. Retrospective Interpretation: Sensemaking is primarily a retrospective process. People make sense of their experiences by reflecting on past events. This means that the meaning of actions and events often becomes clear only after they have occurred.

2. Enactment: Individuals and organizations play an active role in creating their environments. Through their actions and decisions, they enact structures and contexts that shape future experiences. This concept highlights the idea that reality is not just observed but constructed through interaction.

3. Social Process: Sensemaking is inherently social. It involves communication and interaction with others, leading to shared understanding and collective meaning. Organizational culture, norms, and narratives significantly influence this process.

4. Ongoing: Sensemaking is a continuous process. Organizations and individuals are constantly interpreting and reinterpreting their environments as new information and experiences emerge.

5. Extracted Cues: Individuals rely on specific cues or pieces of information to make sense of complex situations. These cues are often drawn from the context and are used to construct a coherent narrative or explanation.

6. Plausibility over Accuracy: In sensemaking, the goal is often to create a plausible narrative rather than an objectively accurate one. This emphasis on plausibility allows for quicker decision-making in uncertain and complex environments.

Practical Application of Sensemaking

Consider a hypothetical case involving FutureTech, a fast-growing tech startup that experiences a sudden drop in employee morale and productivity following a rapid expansion. The leadership team is puzzled by the downturn and needs to understand what went wrong to address the issues effectively.

To engage in sensemaking, the CEO initiates a series of town hall meetings and small group discussions with employees. These interactions are designed to gather diverse perspectives and extract cues about the current state of the organization. Employees share their experiences, concerns, and interpretations of recent changes, providing valuable insights into the underlying issues.

Through these discussions, the leadership team learns that employees feel overwhelmed by the rapid expansion, which has led to increased workloads and a sense of disconnect from the company's mission and values. There is also a perception that the organizational culture has shifted, becoming more impersonal and less supportive.

Armed with this understanding, the CEO and leadership team take steps to address the issues. They implement measures to improve communication, re-establish the company's core values, and provide additional support to employees. For instance, they introduce mentorship programs, create more opportunities for team-building activities, and ensure that managers are more accessible and supportive.

By engaging in sensemaking, FutureTech's leadership can construct a coherent narrative that explains the drop in morale and productivity. This narrative helps them develop targeted strategies to address the problems, rebuild a positive work culture, and guide the organization through its growing pains.

Understanding and applying sensemaking is crucial for today's managers for several reasons:

- Navigating Ambiguity: In a world characterized by rapid change and uncertainty, sensemaking helps managers interpret ambiguous situations and develop coherent strategies. This capability is essential for making informed decisions in complex environments.

- Improving Communication: By recognizing the social nature of sensemaking, managers can foster open communication and dialogue within their organizations. This approach encourages diverse perspectives and collective understanding, enhancing team cohesion and collaboration.

- Building Adaptive Organizations: Sensemaking enables organizations to be more adaptive and responsive to change. By continuously interpreting and reinterpreting their environments, organizations can stay agile and adjust their strategies as needed.

- Enhancing Leadership Effectiveness: Effective leaders are skilled sensemakers. They can articulate a clear and compelling vision, help their teams understand and navigate challenges, and create meaning in times of uncertainty. This ability to construct plausible narratives and guide organizational sensemaking is a key leadership competency.

- Cultivating Organizational Culture: Sensemaking is deeply influenced by organizational culture. Managers who understand this relationship can actively shape and reinforce a culture that supports positive sensemaking, fostering a shared sense of purpose and direction.

EcoMarket, an international retail company, faces a crisis when a major supplier is implicated in unethical labor practices. The news spreads quickly, threatening the company's reputation and stakeholder trust. The CEO initiates a sensemaking process by holding meetings with employees, customers, and suppliers to gather their perspectives and understand the impact of the crisis.

Through these discussions, the leadership team learns that stakeholders are concerned about EcoMarket's commitment to ethical practices and transparency. The CEO uses this feedback to construct a narrative that acknowledges the issue, outlines the steps being taken to address it, and reaffirms the company's dedication to ethical sourcing. This narrative is communicated transparently across all channels, helping to restore trust and guide the organization through the crisis.

By applying Weick's sensemaking principles, EcoMarket not only navigates the immediate crisis but also strengthens its organizational culture and stakeholder relationships, demonstrating the power of sensemaking in managing complex and ambiguous situations. Karl Weick's sensemaking theory offers valuable insights into how organizations can interpret and navigate complex environments. By embracing sensemaking, managers can enhance their decision-making, foster a positive organizational culture, and lead their teams more effectively through uncertainty and change. As we continue exploring core theories and concepts, consider how sensemaking can be applied within your own organization to drive success and resilience.

Resource Dependency Theory (Pfeffer and Salancik)

Resource Dependency Theory, developed by Jeffrey Pfeffer and Gerald Salancik, provides a framework for understanding how organizations manage their dependencies on external resources. The theory posits that organizations are not self-sufficient; they rely on external entities for essential resources such as raw materials, information, technology, and financial capital. This dependency creates power dynamics and strategic behaviors aimed at securing these resources to ensure organizational survival and success.

At its core, Resource Dependency Theory highlights the power imbalances that arise from these dependencies. Organizations depend on external sources for critical resources, and this dependence can create vulnerabilities. The more an organization relies on a particular resource, the more power the supplier of that resource has over the organization. This power can influence organizational behavior, decision-making processes, and strategic choices.

Organizations use various strategies to manage these dependencies and mitigate the associated risks. One common approach is to diversify resource sources, thereby reducing reliance on any single provider. By cultivating multiple suppliers or seeking alternative resources, organizations can lessen their vulnerability and gain greater control over their resource environment.

Another strategy involves forming strategic alliances and partnerships. By collaborating with other organizations, businesses can secure stable access to necessary resources. These alliances might include joint ventures, long-term contracts, or informal networks that provide mutual support. Such relationships help organizations share risks, pool resources, and enhance their collective bargaining power.

Environmental scanning is also crucial in managing resource dependencies. Organizations must continuously monitor their external environment to identify changes that could impact resource availability and stability. By staying informed about market trends, regulatory shifts, and technological advancements, organizations can anticipate potential threats and opportunities, allowing them to adjust their strategies proactively.

Consider a hypothetical case of GreenWave, a nonprofit organization focused on environmental conservation. GreenWave relies heavily on government funding to support its programs. Recently, changes in government policy have threatened this funding, putting GreenWave's financial stability at risk. Recognizing this dependency, the leadership team decides to diversify its funding sources to mitigate the risk.

GreenWave begins by seeking grants from private foundations and philanthropic organizations. They also explore partnerships with corporate sponsors interested in supporting environmental causes. Additionally, GreenWave launches community fundraising campaigns to engage local supporters and generate alternative revenue streams. By diversifying its funding sources, GreenWave reduces its dependency on government funding and secures a more stable financial future.

For modern managers, understanding Resource Dependency Theory is crucial for several reasons. It provides a strategic lens through which to view and manage external relationships and dependencies. By recognizing the power dynamics at play, managers can develop strategies to balance these relationships and ensure a steady flow of essential resources.

The theory emphasizes the importance of adaptability and proactive management. In an ever-changing business environment, managers must be vigilant in monitoring external factors that could impact resource availability. This requires a forward-thinking approach, where managers anticipate changes and develop contingency plans to address potential disruptions.

Resource Dependency Theory (RDT) also underscores the significance of strategic alliances. In a globalized and interconnected economy, collaboration and partnership are often key to securing critical resources and maintaining competitive advantage. Managers who can effectively navigate and leverage these alliances can position their organizations for long-term success.

Hypothetical case examples illustrate the practical application of this theory. Consider BetaHealth, a healthcare provider facing potential shortages in medical supplies due to geopolitical tensions affecting its main supplier. To manage this dependency, BetaHealth establishes relationships with multiple suppliers across different regions, ensuring a steady supply chain. They also invest in developing in-house capabilities to produce certain critical supplies, further reducing their external dependency. In another scenario, EcoMarket, an international retail company specializing in eco-friendly products, forms strategic partnerships with sustainable farms and producers worldwide. By doing so, EcoMarket ensures a reliable supply of ethically sourced products while supporting its brand commitment to sustainability. These partnerships also provide EcoMarket with a competitive edge in the market, attracting customers who prioritize ethical consumption.

Resource Dependency Theory offers valuable insights into the strategic management of external dependencies. By understanding and applying this theory, managers can develop robust strategies to secure essential resources, balance power dynamics, and ensure organizational resilience. As we continue exploring core theories and concepts, consider how managing resource dependencies can enhance your organization's stability and strategic positioning.

Institutional Theory and Legitimacy (Meyer and Rowan)

Institutional Theory, as articulated by scholars John Meyer and Brian Rowan, provides a profound understanding of how organizations conform to societal norms, values, and expectations to gain legitimacy. This theory suggests that organizations are not solely driven by efficiency and productivity but also by the need to align with the institutional environments in which they operate. Legitimacy, in this context, is the perception that an organization's actions are appropriate, proper, and desirable within a given social framework.

Meyer and Rowan's work highlights that organizations adopt formal structures, practices, and procedures that are widely accepted and legitimized within their institutional environments. This process, known as isomorphism, leads organizations to become more similar over time as they adopt common norms and standards. Isomorphism can occur through coercive mechanisms (pressure from regulatory bodies or powerful stakeholders), mimetic processes (imitation of successful organizations), and normative influences (professional standards and cultural expectations).

One key aspect of Institutional Theory is the distinction between technical and institutional environments. In a technical environment, the focus is on efficiency, performance, and measurable outcomes. Organizations operating in such environments prioritize processes and practices that enhance productivity and competitiveness. In contrast, the institutional environment emphasizes conformity to social norms, values, and expectations. Organizations in these environments adopt practices that may not necessarily improve efficiency but are essential for gaining social approval and legitimacy.

The concept of decoupling is also central to Meyer and Rowan's theory. Decoupling refers to the practice where organizations adopt formal structures and practices to appear legitimate to external audiences while their actual operations remain unchanged. This allows organizations to gain legitimacy and support from stakeholders without necessarily altering their core activities.

Consider a hypothetical case involving BetaCo, a retail company specializing in eco-friendly products. To enhance its legitimacy and appeal to environmentally conscious consumers, BetaCo seeks certification as a B Corporation, which requires meeting high standards of social and environmental performance, accountability, and transparency. To achieve this certification, BetaCo undergoes significant changes. They implement sustainable sourcing practices, reduce their carbon footprint, and increase transparency in their supply chain operations. These changes not only align BetaCo with societal expectations but also enhance their brand reputation and attract customers who value sustainability.

In another example, GreenWave, a nonprofit organization focused on environmental conservation, operates in an environment where legitimacy is crucial for securing funding and support. To gain legitimacy, GreenWave aligns its programs with the priorities of major donors and regulatory bodies. They adopt best practices in governance, financial reporting, and program evaluation to demonstrate their accountability and effectiveness. By conforming to these institutional norms, GreenWave gains the trust and support of stakeholders, ensuring continued funding and operational stability.

For modern managers, understanding Institutional Theory and the importance of legitimacy is essential for several reasons. Firstly, it emphasizes the role of social and cultural factors in organizational success. Managers must recognize that gaining legitimacy within their institutional environment is as crucial as achieving technical efficiency. This involves aligning organizational practices with societal values, norms, and expectations.

Secondly, Institutional Theory highlights the need for strategic conformity. Managers must be adept at identifying the key norms and standards within their institutional environment and ensuring that their organizations adhere to these expectations. This might involve adopting industry best practices, pursuing relevant certifications, or engaging in corporate social responsibility initiatives.

Thirdly, the concept of decoupling offers a pragmatic approach to balancing legitimacy and operational effectiveness. Managers can adopt formal structures and practices to meet external legitimacy requirements while maintaining flexibility in their core operations. This allows organizations to navigate institutional pressures without compromising their efficiency and productivity.

In today's globalized and interconnected world, where public perception and social responsibility play an increasingly significant role, the insights from Institutional Theory are more relevant than ever. Managers must be skilled at navigating the complex landscape of institutional expectations and leveraging legitimacy to build trust, enhance reputation, and ensure long-term success.

Meyer and Rowan's Institutional Theory and the concept of legitimacy provide a comprehensive framework for understanding the social dimensions of organizational behavior. By embracing these principles, managers can align their organizations with societal norms, gain legitimacy, and build sustainable relationships with stakeholders. As we continue exploring core theories and concepts, consider how institutional alignment and legitimacy can enhance your organization's strategic positioning and overall success.

In today's dynamic and interconnected business environment, understanding and applying modern organizational theories is not just beneficial; it is essential for effective management. Each theory offers unique insights that help managers navigate the complexities of organizational life, adapt to change, and achieve strategic objectives.

Rational, Natural, and Open Systems perspectives provide a comprehensive understanding of organizational structures and processes. By balancing the efficiency-focused approach of rational systems with the human-centric view of natural systems and the adaptability of open systems, managers can create more resilient and responsive organizations.

Bounded Rationality and Satisficing highlight the limitations of human decision-making. By recognizing these constraints, managers can set realistic expectations, streamline decision-making processes, and develop supportive systems that enhance performance without overburdening employees.

Sensemaking in Organizations emphasizes the importance of interpreting and navigating complex environments. Managers who excel in sensemaking can foster a culture of continuous learning and adaptation, guiding their teams through uncertainty and change with clarity and confidence.

Resource Dependency Theory underscores the strategic importance of managing external dependencies. By diversifying resource sources, forming strategic alliances, and proactively scanning the environment, managers can secure critical resources, mitigate risks, and maintain competitive advantage.

Institutional Theory and Legitimacy stress the need for organizations to align with societal norms and expectations. Managers who understand the importance of legitimacy can build trust with stakeholders, enhance organizational reputation, and ensure long-term sustainability by adopting practices that resonate with their institutional environment.

By understanding and applying these theories, managers can develop more adaptable, resilient, and effective organizations. Whether it is through optimizing organizational structures, enhancing decision-making processes, fostering a positive culture, managing external dependencies, or aligning with societal expectations, these theories provide the insights needed to navigate the complexities of today's business world. Embracing these modern theories is not merely an academic exercise but a strategic imperative for any manager seeking to lead a high-performing and sustainable organization. As we continue our journey through organizational theory, keep these concepts in mind and consider how they can be leveraged to drive success in your own organization.

Part II: Organizational Structure and Design

Part II: Organizational Structure and Design explores the fundamental aspects of how organizations are structured and the principles that guide their design. This section provides a comprehensive understanding of the different types of organizational structures, the strategic alignment necessary for effective design, and the dynamic interplay between structure, strategy, and technology.

Understanding organizational structure is crucial as it defines the framework within which an organization operates. The types of structures, whether hierarchical, flat, matrix, or networked, each come with distinct advantages and challenges. By examining these various structures, managers can better appreciate how organizational form impacts efficiency, communication, and decision-making processes.

A key distinction in organizational structure is between mechanistic and organic structures. Mechanistic structures are characterized by rigid hierarchies, fixed duties, and a high degree of formalization, making them suitable for stable environments where efficiency and predictability are paramount. Conversely, organic structures are more flexible, with decentralized decision-making and adaptive roles, thriving in dynamic environments that demand innovation and responsiveness.

Karl Weick's concept of loosely coupled systems offers another perspective on organizational design. Loosely coupled systems are characterized by components that retain some independence while still being part of the larger organizational framework. This allows for adaptability and resilience, as changes in one part of the system do not necessarily disrupt the entire organization.

Designing effective organizations goes beyond selecting the appropriate structure; it involves aligning the structure with the organization's strategy. Strategic alignment ensures that the organizational design supports the overall goals and objectives, enabling better performance and competitive advantage. This alignment requires a deep understanding of how various elements of the organization fit together and contribute to its mission.

Decentralization and complexity are critical considerations in organizational design. Decentralization distributes decision-making authority closer to the front lines, enhancing responsiveness and empowering employees. However, it also introduces complexity that must be managed carefully to avoid fragmentation and inefficiencies. Understanding how to balance these elements is key to creating a cohesive and effective organization.

The impact of technology on organizational design cannot be overstated. Technological advancements have transformed how organizations operate, communicate, and compete. Technology enables new forms of organizational structure, such as virtual teams and remote work arrangements, and necessitates continuous adaptation to remain effective. By embracing technology and integrating it into the design process, organizations can enhance agility, innovation, and productivity. In this section, we will explore these themes in detail, providing insights and practical examples to help managers design organizations that are not only efficient and effective but also adaptable and resilient in the face of change. Through this exploration, we aim to equip you with the knowledge and tools to create structures that support strategic objectives, foster innovation, and leverage the full potential of your organization's capabilities.

Chapter 3: Understanding Organizational Structure

Organizational structure defines how tasks are divided, coordinated, and supervised within an organization. The structure chosen by an organization impacts its efficiency, communication, and adaptability. Here, we explore several common types of organizational structures, each with its unique characteristics, advantages, and challenges.

Hierarchical Structure

A hierarchical structure, also known as a tall structure, is the most traditional and widely recognized form. It features multiple levels of management, with a clear chain of command extending from top executives down to front-line employees. Each level in the hierarchy controls the level below and is accountable to the level above.

In this structure, roles and responsibilities are clearly defined, which can lead to greater clarity and efficiency in decision-making processes. However, the rigidity of a hierarchical structure can stifle innovation and slow down response times, as decisions often need to pass through multiple layers of management. This type of structure is commonly found in large, established organizations with stable environments, such as government agencies and large corporations.

Flat Structure

A flat structure, or horizontal structure, reduces the number of management layers, creating a more direct line of communication between employees and top management. This structure is characterized by a broad span of control, where managers oversee a larger number of employees directly.

The primary advantage of a flat structure is increased flexibility and faster decision-making, as there are fewer layers for information to pass through. It also fosters a more collaborative and inclusive work environment, empowering employees by giving them more responsibility and autonomy. However, this structure can lead to challenges in managing and coordinating large teams, potentially resulting in overburdened managers and unclear reporting relationships.

Matrix Structure

A matrix structure combines elements of both hierarchical and flat structures, creating a grid-like arrangement where employees report to multiple managers. Typically, this involves dual reporting lines: one to a functional manager (e.g., head of marketing) and another to a project or product manager.

This structure is designed to enhance flexibility and collaboration, allowing organizations to leverage specialized skills across different projects and departments. It can lead to more dynamic and innovative solutions, as employees collaborate across functional boundaries. However, the complexity of dual reporting lines can create confusion and conflicts, requiring strong communication and conflict-resolution skills to manage effectively. Matrix structures are often used in industries like consulting, aerospace, and engineering, where cross-functional teamwork is essential.

Divisional Structure

A divisional structure organizes the company around products, services, or geographical areas. Each division operates semi-autonomously, with its own resources and management structure, but remains connected to the overall corporate strategy and objectives.

This structure allows for greater focus and specialization within each division, enabling quicker responses to market changes and customer needs. It also fosters accountability and performance measurement at the divisional level. However, it can lead to duplication of resources and efforts, as each division may have its own functional departments. Additionally, divisions might operate in silos, hindering cross-division collaboration and sharing of best practices. Divisional structures are commonly found in large, diversified companies with multiple product lines or regional markets, such as multinational corporations.

Network Structure

A network structure, also known as a virtual organization, relies on a central core with various functions outsourced to external entities. This type of structure is highly flexible and can adapt quickly to changes in the environment by leveraging external partnerships and resources.

The primary advantage of a network structure is its agility and ability to scale operations up or down based on demand. It reduces overhead costs and allows the organization to focus on its core competencies while outsourcing non-core activities. However, managing and coordinating a network of external partners can be challenging, requiring strong relationship management and effective communication. This structure is often used by technology companies, startups, and organizations in fast-paced industries.

Hybrid Structure

A hybrid structure incorporates elements from various organizational structures to create a system that meets the specific needs of the organization. It might combine aspects of hierarchical, flat, matrix, and divisional structures, allowing for a tailored approach that leverages the strengths of each model while mitigating their weaknesses.

Hybrid structures provide the flexibility to adapt to different business units' unique requirements and the overarching organizational strategy. However, the complexity of managing a hybrid structure can be high, requiring careful planning and clear communication to ensure coherence and alignment across the organization.

Team-Based Structure

A team-based structure organizes the company around teams rather than traditional departments or functions. Teams are formed to address specific projects or tasks, and members are often cross-functional, bringing diverse skills and perspectives.

This structure enhances collaboration, innovation, and speed in addressing tasks, as teams can be more responsive and agile. It fosters a sense of ownership and accountability among team members. However, the constant formation and dissolution of teams can create instability and challenges in maintaining consistent organizational practices. It requires strong leadership and clear goals to ensure teams remain aligned with the overall organizational objectives.

In summary, the type of organizational structure adopted by a company significantly influences its operations, communication, and overall effectiveness. Each structure has its advantages and challenges, and the choice of structure should align with the organization's strategy, goals, and environmental context. By understanding these various structures, managers can design their organizations to optimize performance, foster innovation, and adapt to changing conditions.

Holacratic Structure

A holacratic organization represents a radical departure from traditional hierarchical structures, embracing a decentralized approach to management and decision-making. Developed by Brian Robertson, holacracy distributes authority and decision-making throughout self-organizing teams rather than concentrating it in a management hierarchy.

In a holacratic organization, traditional job titles and rigid reporting lines are replaced by dynamic roles defined by responsibilities and accountabilities. These roles are grouped into circles, which are semi-autonomous teams responsible for specific functions or projects. Each circle operates independently but aligns with the broader organizational purpose and goals.

Decision-making authority is decentralized to individuals within their roles, empowering employees at all levels. Roles are flexible and can be redefined as needed, allowing employees to hold multiple roles with clear responsibilities that evolve with the organization's needs. Holacratic organizations use formal governance processes to define and adjust roles, policies, and structures through regular meetings. Tactical meetings focus on addressing operational issues and coordinating activities.

Holacracy promotes transparency by making information and decision-making processes accessible to all members, ensuring accountability through clear role definitions and regular feedback. This structure can increase agility, innovation, and employee engagement by allowing organizations to respond quickly to changes and leverage collective intelligence. Employees feel more empowered and motivated, having greater control over their work. However, transitioning to holacracy requires a significant cultural shift and commitment. The formal processes involved can be time-consuming and require discipline, and not all employees may thrive in such a decentralized and evolving environment.

Mechanistic and organic structures represent two distinct approaches to organizational design, each suited to different types of environments and organizational goals.

Mechanistic Structures

Mechanistic structures are highly formalized and centralized, characterized by a clear hierarchy, rigid departmentalization, and a narrow span of control. Roles and responsibilities are well-defined, and communication follows strict, vertical channels. Decision-making authority is concentrated at the top levels of the hierarchy, and standardized procedures and rules govern activities.

This type of structure is typically found in organizations operating in stable, predictable environments where efficiency and consistency are paramount. Mechanistic structures excel in industries such as manufacturing, where tasks are routine and the focus is on precision and optimization. The rigidity of mechanistic structures ensures that everyone knows their role and follows established protocols, which helps maintain control and order.

Organic Structures

Organic structures, on the other hand, are characterized by a more flexible and decentralized approach. They feature a flat hierarchy, wide spans of control, and a fluid arrangement of roles and responsibilities. Communication flows more freely, often laterally, and decision-making is distributed throughout the organization. This allows for greater adaptability and innovation, as employees at all levels are empowered to respond quickly to changes and challenges.

Organic structures thrive in dynamic and uncertain environments where flexibility and creativity are essential. They are commonly found in industries like technology and startups, where rapid change and the need for constant innovation are the norms. By fostering a collaborative and adaptive culture, organic structures enable organizations to leverage the diverse skills and insights of their workforce.

Consider a traditional manufacturing company, ClassicAuto, which utilizes a mechanistic structure. In ClassicAuto, each department has specific roles, and employees follow established procedures to ensure the production process is efficient and consistent. The centralized decision-making process helps maintain control and predictability, essential for managing large-scale manufacturing operations.

In contrast, a tech startup like Innovatech adopts an organic structure. At Innovatech, roles are flexible, and teams are encouraged to collaborate across departments. Decision-making authority is distributed, allowing employees to experiment with new ideas and respond rapidly to market changes. This flexibility fosters innovation and helps Innovatech stay competitive in the fast-paced tech industry.

The choice between mechanistic and organic structures depends on the organization's environment and strategic objectives. Mechanistic structures provide stability and efficiency in predictable settings, while organic structures offer flexibility and adaptability in dynamic environments. Understanding the strengths and limitations of each approach helps managers design organizations that are well-suited to their specific operational contexts.

Hybrid Structures

Many modern organizations adopt a hybrid or mechan-organic structure, which combines elements of both mechanistic and organic designs. This approach allows organizations to balance the need for stability and efficiency with the flexibility and adaptability required to thrive in changing environments.

A hybrid structure maintains some degree of hierarchical control and formalization for core functions that benefit from consistency and standardization, such as finance, HR, and operations. At the same time, it incorporates more flexible, team-based approaches for areas that require innovation and rapid response, such as research and development, marketing, and customer service.

TechAuto, an automotive company that blends traditional manufacturing with cutting-edge technology, adopts a hybrid structure. TechAuto maintains a mechanistic approach in its manufacturing division to ensure high levels of efficiency and quality control. Here, roles are clearly defined, and processes are standardized to maintain consistency.

Simultaneously, TechAuto's research and development (R&D) and marketing divisions operate with an organic structure. These teams are given the flexibility to innovate and respond quickly to market trends and technological advancements. Cross-functional teams in these areas collaborate freely, with a more decentralized decision-making process that encourages creativity and rapid iteration.

By combining mechanistic and organic elements, TechAuto can leverage the efficiency and control of a mechanistic structure where stability is crucial, while also benefiting from the adaptability and innovation fostered by an organic approach in areas that demand flexibility.

Hybrid structures offer several benefits, including enhanced flexibility, improved innovation, and balanced control. Organizations can allocate resources more efficiently, apply formal controls where necessary, and empower teams to drive innovation and responsiveness. However, managing a hybrid structure can also present challenges. Balancing the differing needs of mechanistic and organic components requires careful coordination and communication. Leaders must be adept at fostering a culture that supports both stability and flexibility, ensuring that the organization can operate efficiently while remaining agile.

Hybrid structures provide a versatile approach to organizational design, enabling organizations to leverage the strengths of both mechanistic and organic structures. By understanding and implementing a hybrid approach, managers can create organizations that are efficient, innovative, and adaptable, well-equipped to navigate the complexities of modern business environments.

Loosely Coupled Systems (Weick)

Karl Weick's concept of loosely coupled systems offers a unique perspective on organizational structure and design. Loosely coupled systems are characterized by elements that are relatively independent yet still connected in ways that allow them to respond to and influence each other. This balance between independence and interdependence creates a structure that is flexible and adaptable while maintaining a cohesive overall system.

In a loosely coupled system, the components or units of an organization—such as departments, teams, or processes—operate with a degree of autonomy. These units can pursue their own goals and make decisions independently, which allows for greater flexibility and responsiveness to local conditions. However, despite this autonomy, the units are still part of a larger organizational framework, connected through shared goals, values, and information channels.

Key Characteristics of Loosely Coupled Systems

- Autonomy and Flexibility: Units within a loosely coupled system have the freedom to adapt and respond to changes in their immediate environment without requiring approval from higher levels of the organization. This autonomy allows for quick decision-making and innovation at the local level.

- Interconnectedness: While units operate independently, they are still connected by overarching goals, values, and information systems. This interconnectedness ensures that the organization remains cohesive and aligned despite the independence of its parts.

- Resilience and Adaptability: Loosely coupled systems are inherently resilient because the failure or disruption in one unit does not necessarily impact the entire organization. This structure allows the organization to adapt more easily to changes and disruptions in the environment.

- Reduced Coordination Costs: By allowing units to operate independently, loosely coupled systems can reduce the need for extensive coordination and communication, which can lower operational costs and increase efficiency.

Practical Application of Loosely Coupled Systems

Consider a hypothetical case of EduInnovate, a network of charter schools that adopts a loosely coupled system. Each school within the network operates with significant autonomy, allowing them to tailor their educational programs to meet the specific needs of their students and communities. For instance, one school might focus on STEM education, while another emphasizes the arts.

Despite their autonomy, the schools in the EduInnovate network are connected through a shared mission of providing high-quality education and a central administrative body that handles common functions such as funding, regulatory compliance, and professional development. This structure allows each school to innovate and adapt to local conditions while benefiting from the resources and support of the larger network.

Another example is a multinational corporation like GlobalTech, which operates with a loosely coupled structure. Each regional office has the autonomy to make decisions based on local market conditions, customer preferences, and regulatory environments. For instance, the European office might develop products that cater to the unique tastes and regulations of the European market, while the Asian office focuses on innovations that meet the needs of Asian consumers.

These regional offices are connected by GlobalTech's corporate values, strategic goals, and centralized functions such as R&D, finance, and HR. This loosely coupled structure enables GlobalTech to remain agile and responsive to diverse market conditions while maintaining overall strategic coherence and leveraging shared resources.

The primary benefit of loosely coupled systems is their ability to balance flexibility and control. By granting autonomy to units, organizations can foster innovation and responsiveness, which is particularly valuable in dynamic and complex environments. The interconnectedness of the system ensures that the organization remains aligned and cohesive, even as individual units pursue their specific goals.

Managing a loosely coupled system can also present challenges. Ensuring effective communication and coordination across independent units requires robust information systems and a strong shared culture. There is also a risk of misalignment if units diverge too far from the organization's overall mission and goals. Leaders must carefully manage the balance between autonomy and interconnectedness to maintain coherence and strategic direction. Karl Weick's concept of loosely coupled systems offers a powerful framework for designing organizations that are both flexible and resilient. By allowing units to operate independently while maintaining connections through shared goals and values, loosely coupled systems can adapt to change and innovate effectively. Understanding and applying this concept helps managers create organizations that are agile, responsive, and well-equipped to navigate the complexities of today's business environment.

Organizational structure is a fundamental aspect of business management that determines how tasks are divided, coordinated, and supervised. This chapter has explored various organizational structures—mechanistic, organic, hybrid, and loosely coupled systems—each offering unique advantages and challenges.

Mechanistic structures, with their clear hierarchies and rigid protocols, excel in stable environments where efficiency and predictability are crucial. Organic structures, characterized by flexibility and decentralized decision-making, thrive in dynamic settings where innovation and rapid response are essential. Hybrid structures combine elements of both mechanistic and organic designs, allowing organizations to balance stability with adaptability.

Karl Weick's concept of loosely coupled systems introduces an innovative perspective, highlighting the balance between autonomy and interconnectedness. Loosely coupled systems are particularly valuable in complex and rapidly changing environments, offering resilience and adaptability while maintaining overall organizational coherence.

As business professionals, the practical application of these theories can significantly enhance organizational effectiveness.

Here are some practical considerations for implementing these structures in your organization:

1. Assess Your Environment: The choice of structure should align with your organizational environment. If your industry is stable and efficiency-driven, a mechanistic structure might be appropriate. Conversely, if you operate in a fast-paced, innovative sector, an organic structure could be more beneficial.

2. Balance Stability and Flexibility: Hybrid structures offer a balanced approach, combining the stability of mechanistic elements with the flexibility of organic components. Consider which areas of your organization require tight control and which can benefit from more autonomy.

3. Foster Innovation and Responsiveness: Implementing loosely coupled systems can enhance your organization's ability to innovate and respond to changes. Encourage autonomy in teams and departments while maintaining alignment through shared goals and robust communication channels.

4. Leverage Technology: The impact of technology on organizational design cannot be overstated. Use advanced information systems to facilitate communication, coordination, and decision-making across different parts of your organization. Technology can help bridge the gap between autonomous units and ensure cohesive operation.

5. Cultivate a Strong Organizational Culture: Regardless of the structure, a strong organizational culture is essential. Shared values, clear mission, and consistent communication foster unity and alignment, even in the most decentralized or loosely coupled systems.

6. Regularly Review and Adapt: Organizational structures should not be static. Regularly assess your structure's effectiveness and make adjustments as needed. This continuous improvement mindset ensures that your

organization remains agile and responsive to both internal and external changes.

Understanding and strategically applying these organizational structures can transform how your business operates. By choosing the right structure, fostering a culture of innovation, leveraging technology, and maintaining flexibility, you can create an organization that is not only efficient and effective but also resilient and adaptive in today's complex business landscape. As we move forward to the next chapter on designing effective organizations, keep these foundational concepts in mind. The ability to align structure with strategy, navigate decentralization and complexity, and integrate technological advancements will be critical in building organizations that thrive in the modern world. Let's explore how these principles can be practically implemented to drive your organization's success.

Chapter 4: Designing Effective Organizations

Imagine a symphony orchestra preparing for a grand performance. Each musician, from the violinist to the percussionist, plays a unique role. Their individual efforts, however, must be perfectly coordinated and aligned with the conductor's vision to create a harmonious masterpiece. Similarly, in the business world, an organization's structure must be meticulously designed to align with its strategic goals, ensuring that every department and team works in concert to achieve excellence.

Designing effective organizations is about more than just assigning roles and responsibilities. It's about creating a framework that supports the organization's strategic objectives, facilitates efficient decision-making, and fosters an environment conducive to innovation and adaptability. This chapter will delve into the critical aspects of organizational design, exploring how structure, decentralization, and technology can be leveraged to build dynamic and resilient organizations.

Aligning structure with strategy is the cornerstone of effective organizational design. Just as a well-orchestrated performance requires each musician to understand their part and how it fits into the whole, aligning an organization's structure with its strategy ensures that every team and individual is working towards common goals. This alignment creates a seamless connection between strategic vision and operational execution, enabling the organization to move forward with clarity and purpose.

Decentralization and complexity introduce another layer of consideration in organizational design. In today's fast-paced and unpredictable business environment, the ability to respond quickly to changes and make decisions at the local level is invaluable. Decentralization empowers employees, fosters innovation, and enhances agility, but it also brings complexity that must be carefully managed. Balancing the benefits of decentralization with the need for coherence and control is a delicate act, akin to ensuring that the diverse instruments in an orchestra remain in sync while allowing for moments of individual brilliance.

The impact of technology on organizational design cannot be overstated. As technological advancements continue to reshape the business landscape, organizations must adapt their structures to leverage these innovations. Technology enables new forms of collaboration, communication, and information sharing, breaking down traditional barriers and creating more fluid and adaptive structures. From virtual teams to AI-driven decision-making tools, technology offers countless opportunities to enhance organizational design and performance.

We will explore how these elements come together to create effective organizations. We will examine the principles of aligning structure with strategy, the intricacies of managing decentralization and complexity, and the transformative role of technology in organizational design. Through practical insights and illustrative examples, we aim to provide a comprehensive guide for managers and leaders striving to build organizations that are not only efficient and effective but also resilient and adaptable in the face of change.

Join us as we embark on this journey to understand the art and science of designing organizations that can thrive in today's dynamic and complex business environment. Whether you are leading a small startup or a large multinational corporation, the principles and practices discussed in this chapter will equip you with the tools to design a structure that supports your strategic vision and drives your organization towards sustained success.

Aligning structure with strategy is a critical aspect of effective organizational design. It ensures that the way an organization is structured supports its strategic objectives, enabling it to achieve its goals more efficiently and effectively. This alignment involves matching the organization's structure with its strategy to ensure coherence and synergy across all levels.

An organization's strategy defines its long-term goals and the actions needed to achieve them. The structure, on the other hand, determines how these actions are organized, coordinated, and executed. When structure and strategy are aligned, the organization operates smoothly, with clear communication channels, efficient workflows, and a cohesive effort toward common objectives.

For instance, a company pursuing a cost leadership strategy, aiming to be the lowest-cost producer in its industry, might benefit from a mechanistic structure. This structure, with its clear hierarchies, standardized procedures, and tight control mechanisms, can help minimize costs and maximize efficiency. By having well-defined roles and responsibilities, the organization can streamline operations and reduce waste, directly supporting its strategic goal of cost leadership.

Conversely, a company focused on innovation and differentiation may thrive with an organic structure. Such a structure, characterized by flexibility, decentralized decision-making, and collaborative environments, fosters creativity and rapid adaptation. This setup allows the organization to respond quickly to market changes, experiment with new ideas, and bring innovative products to market faster, aligning perfectly with a strategy centered on differentiation.

In dynamic and competitive industries, many organizations adopt a hybrid structure to balance the need for efficiency with the need for flexibility. This approach allows different parts of the organization to operate with varying degrees of centralization and autonomy, depending on their specific roles and objectives. For example, while the core operations might be structured mechanistically to ensure reliability and cost control, the research and development department might follow a more organic model to encourage innovation.

Aligning structure with strategy also involves considering the external environment. In rapidly changing markets, an organization's ability to adapt its structure to emerging opportunities and threats is crucial. This might involve shifting from a more hierarchical to a more decentralized structure to improve responsiveness. The use of cross-functional teams, agile methodologies, and project-based structures can enhance the organization's ability to pivot quickly in response to environmental changes.

Additionally, technology plays a significant role in aligning structure with strategy. Advanced information systems can facilitate better communication and coordination across different parts of the organization. These systems enable real-time data sharing and collaboration, breaking down silos and ensuring that all units are aligned with the overall strategic direction.

Leadership commitment is essential in aligning structure with strategy. Leaders must clearly communicate the strategic vision and ensure that the organizational structure is designed to support this vision. This involves regular reviews and adjustments to the structure to keep it aligned with evolving strategic goals. Leaders should also foster a culture that embraces change and encourages continuous improvement, as this cultural alignment can significantly enhance the effectiveness of structural alignment.

Aligning structure with strategy is about creating a harmonious relationship between an organization's long-term goals and its operational framework. By ensuring that the structure supports strategic objectives, organizations can achieve greater efficiency, adaptability, and overall effectiveness. This alignment requires a thoughtful consideration of the organization's goals, environment, and the role of technology, supported by strong leadership and a culture of continuous improvement.

Decentralization and Complexity

Decentralization, the distribution of decision-making authority to lower levels in an organization, is a powerful approach for fostering agility, innovation, and responsiveness. In contrast to centralized structures, where decisions are made at the top and flow down through rigid hierarchies, decentralized organizations empower individuals and teams at various levels to make decisions that affect their work. This shift can dramatically enhance an organization's ability to respond quickly to changes, capitalize on new opportunities, and address local challenges effectively.

The primary advantage of decentralization is its ability to enhance flexibility and speed. In a decentralized structure, decisions are made closer to the action, where detailed knowledge and contextual understanding are greatest. For instance, in a global company, regional managers can make market-specific decisions without waiting for approval from headquarters, allowing the company to adapt swiftly to local market conditions. This responsiveness is crucial in fast-paced industries like technology, where the ability to pivot quickly can be the difference between success and failure.

- Decentralization fosters innovation by creating an environment where employees are encouraged to take initiative and experiment with new ideas. When individuals at all levels are empowered to make decisions, they are more likely to feel a sense of ownership and motivation. This can lead to a more dynamic and creative organizational culture. For example, in a tech startup, developers who have the autonomy to explore new solutions and technologies can drive innovation more effectively than in a rigidly controlled environment.

- Decentralization introduces complexity that must be managed carefully. One of the significant challenges is ensuring coherence and alignment across the organization. With decision-making spread across various levels, there is a risk that different parts of the organization may pursue divergent goals or adopt inconsistent practices. Effective communication and strong leadership are essential to maintain a unified direction and ensure that decentralized decisions support the overall strategic objectives.

- Decentralization demands a high level of trust and competency among employees. Empowering individuals to make decisions requires confidence in their abilities and judgment. Investing in training and development is crucial to equip employees with the skills and knowledge needed to make informed decisions. Moreover, fostering a culture of trust and accountability ensures that employees feel supported and are encouraged to act in the organization's best interest.

There are several challenges, for example, potential for duplication of efforts and inefficiencies. Without central oversight, different units might independently undertake similar initiatives, leading to wasted resources. Establishing clear guidelines, accountability mechanisms, and collaborative platforms can help mitigate these risks. For instance, a decentralized company might implement regular cross-departmental meetings and shared databases to ensure that teams are aligned, and resources are used efficiently.

The hybrid approach often emerges as a solution to balance the benefits of decentralization with the need for control and coordination. In such structures, strategic decisions and core functions may remain centralized to maintain consistency and alignment, while operational decisions are decentralized to enhance responsiveness and innovation. For example, a multinational corporation might centralize its strategic planning and financial controls while decentralizing marketing and product development to adapt to regional markets.

Technological advancements play a critical role in managing the complexity associated with decentralization. Modern communication and collaboration tools, such as project management software, cloud-based platforms, and video conferencing, facilitate seamless interaction and information sharing across decentralized units. These technologies enable real-time coordination and oversight, helping to maintain coherence and alignment even in a dispersed organizational structure.

Consider the case of GlobalRetail, a company that has successfully implemented a decentralized structure. Regional managers have the authority to make decisions tailored to their markets, from product offerings to marketing strategies. This autonomy allows GlobalRetail to be highly responsive to local consumer preferences and competitive dynamics. To manage the complexity, GlobalRetail uses an integrated IT system that provides visibility into regional operations and facilitates communication between headquarters and regional offices. Regular strategy sessions and shared performance metrics ensure that all units are aligned with the company's overall objectives.

Decentralization can significantly enhance an organization's agility, innovation, and responsiveness by distributing decision-making authority. However, it introduces complexity that requires careful management through effective communication, strong leadership, clear guidelines, and the strategic use of technology. By balancing decentralization with central oversight, organizations can harness the benefits of both approaches, creating a dynamic and adaptable structure that supports sustained success in a complex and rapidly changing business environment.

The rapid advancement of technology has fundamentally transformed organizational design, reshaping how companies structure their operations, communicate, and compete. Technology enables new forms of collaboration, enhances flexibility, and drives efficiency, allowing organizations to innovate and adapt in ways that were previously unimaginable.

One of the most significant impacts of technology on organizational design is the facilitation of remote work and virtual teams. With advanced communication tools, cloud-based platforms, and collaboration software, employees can work together seamlessly from different locations around the globe. This capability has given rise to more decentralized and flexible organizational structures, where physical presence is no longer a constraint. Companies can tap into a global talent pool, reduce overhead costs associated with maintaining large office spaces, and provide employees with the flexibility to work in environments that maximize their productivity.

Technology also enhances information flow and decision-making processes within organizations. Real-time data analytics and business intelligence tools provide managers with instant access to critical information, enabling more informed and timely decisions. This access to real-time data breaks down silos, ensuring that information is shared across departments and levels of the organization, fostering a more integrated and responsive structure. For example, a retail company can use data analytics to track sales trends and inventory levels in real-time, allowing regional managers to make swift decisions on stock replenishment and promotional strategies.

Automation and artificial intelligence (AI) are transforming organizational roles and workflows. Routine tasks that once required significant human intervention can now be automated, freeing up employees to focus on higher-value activities. AI-driven systems can handle customer service inquiries, manage supply chains, and even assist in decision-making by providing predictive analytics and insights. This shift not only improves efficiency but also necessitates a redesign of organizational roles and responsibilities. Employees need to adapt to new technologies and develop skills that complement automated processes, such as strategic thinking, problem-solving, and interpersonal communication.

The integration of technology also supports the development of more agile and adaptive organizational structures. Agile methodologies, originally developed for software development, have been adopted across various industries to enhance flexibility and responsiveness. These methodologies promote iterative work processes, cross-functional teams, and continuous feedback, allowing organizations to quickly adapt to changes and deliver value to customers more efficiently. For instance, a marketing department might use agile principles to rapidly test and iterate on campaign ideas, ensuring that their strategies remain relevant and effective in a fast-changing market. Technology enables enhanced collaboration and innovation through the use of digital platforms and tools. Platforms like Slack, Microsoft Teams, and Asana facilitate real-time communication and project management, breaking down barriers between departments and promoting a culture of collaboration. Innovation hubs and virtual labs allow teams to experiment with new ideas, share knowledge, and develop innovative solutions, regardless of geographical constraints.

The integration of technology into organizational design also presents challenges. The rapid pace of technological change requires organizations to continuously update their systems and processes, which can be resource intensive. There is also the need for ongoing training and development to ensure that employees possess the necessary skills to leverage new technologies effectively. Furthermore, the reliance on digital tools raises concerns about data security and privacy, necessitating robust cybersecurity measures and protocols.

Consider the case of FinTech Solutions, a financial technology company that has embraced a technology-driven organizational design. FinTech Solutions employs a decentralized structure, with teams distributed across multiple locations. Advanced communication tools and cloud-based platforms enable seamless collaboration among these teams. The company leverages AI and automation to manage routine financial transactions and customer inquiries, allowing employees to focus on developing innovative financial products. Real-time data analytics provide insights that drive strategic decisions, ensuring that the company remains agile and competitive in a rapidly evolving industry.

Technology has a profound impact on organizational design, enabling more flexible, efficient, and innovative structures. By facilitating remote work, enhancing information flow, automating routine tasks, and supporting agile methodologies, technology empowers organizations to adapt quickly to changes and maintain a competitive edge. However, to fully realize these benefits, organizations must invest in continuous learning, robust security measures, and adaptable systems that can evolve with technological advancements. As we navigate this digital era, the ability to integrate technology seamlessly into organizational design will be a key determinant of success.

To effectively design organizations that leverage the power of technology, managers should focus on creating flexible and adaptive structures. Begin by fostering a culture of continuous learning where employees are encouraged to develop new skills that complement technological advancements. Invest in training programs and provide resources that help employees stay current with the latest tools and trends. This proactive approach ensures that the workforce remains capable and confident in navigating the digital landscape.

Embrace remote work and virtual teams as a permanent fixture in your organizational design. Utilize advanced communication and collaboration tools to maintain connectivity and cohesion among geographically dispersed teams. Regular virtual meetings, clear communication channels, and collaborative platforms can help maintain a sense of unity and purpose, even when teams are not physically co-located.

Incorporate data-driven decision-making processes to enhance responsiveness and agility. Utilize real-time data analytics and business intelligence tools to gather insights that inform strategic decisions. By embedding these tools into your organizational processes, you can ensure that decisions are based on accurate and up-to-date information, enhancing overall effectiveness.

Automation and AI should be integrated thoughtfully into workflows to enhance efficiency without sacrificing the human touch. Identify routine and repetitive tasks that can be automated, freeing up employees to focus on more strategic and creative endeavors. This shift not only improves productivity but also increases job satisfaction as employees engage in more meaningful work.

Adopt agile methodologies across various departments to promote flexibility and innovation. Agile principles such as iterative work processes, cross-functional teams, and continuous feedback can be applied beyond software development to areas like marketing, product development, and operations. This approach helps organizations quickly adapt to changes and continuously improve their processes and outputs.

Ensure robust cybersecurity measures to protect data and maintain trust. As technology becomes more integral to organizational design, safeguarding information becomes paramount. Implement strong security protocols, conduct regular audits, and educate employees on best practices for data security.

The integration of technology into organizational design offers numerous benefits, including increased flexibility, efficiency, and innovation. By aligning structure with strategy, embracing decentralization, and leveraging technological advancements, organizations can create dynamic and resilient frameworks capable of thriving in today's fast-paced environment. The practical advice provided throughout this chapter equips managers with the tools needed to design organizations that not only meet current demands but are also prepared for future challenges. As you move forward, keep these principles in mind and continuously seek ways to refine and enhance your organizational design to stay competitive and effective in the digital age.

Part III: Organizational Processes and Dynamics

Organizations are not static entities; they are dynamic systems that evolve through complex interactions and processes. Part III of this book explores the intricate workings of organizational processes and dynamics, offering insights into how decisions are made, power is wielded, and political landscapes are navigated within companies. Understanding these elements is crucial for anyone looking to lead, manage, or thrive in a business environment.

Decision-making is at the heart of organizational activity. Every day, countless decisions shape the direction and success of a business. In this section, we explore various theories and models that explain how decisions are made within organizations. We begin with the Behavioral Theory of the Firm by Cyert and March, which provides a nuanced view of decision-making as a process influenced by bounded rationality, organizational goals, and the interactions of different stakeholders. Next, we examine the Garbage Can Model of Organizational Choice, which presents a more chaotic and fluid perspective, highlighting how decisions can emerge in an environment of ambiguity and varying priorities. We also enquire into the role of political language and symbols, illustrating how communication and symbolism can shape and influence decision-making processes.

Power, politics, and influence are omnipresent in organizational life. They determine how decisions are made, who gets to make them, and how resources are allocated. In the section on power and politics, we explore the various sources and types of power within organizations. Understanding these sources—whether they stem from formal authority, expertise, or relationships—provides a foundation for navigating and managing organizational dynamics. We also discuss political strategies and tactics, offering practical insights into how individuals and groups can effectively use political skills to achieve their objectives. Managing organizational politics involves recognizing and addressing the often-unspoken influences that affect decision-making and organizational behavior.

This part of the book aims to equip you with a deeper understanding of the processes and dynamics that drive organizations. By exploring decision-making theories, power structures, and political strategies, we provide a comprehensive toolkit for navigating the complexities of organizational life. Whether you are a manager seeking to make better decisions, a leader aiming to wield influence more effectively, or an employee striving to understand the political landscape of your workplace, the insights and strategies presented here will help you thrive in the dynamic environment of modern organizations.

Chapter 5: Decision-Making in Organizations

Decision-making lies at the heart of organizational life, shaping the direction, strategy, and daily operations of any business. Whether it's a multinational corporation planning its global strategy or a small startup navigating market entry, the way decisions are made can significantly impact an organization's success and resilience. Understanding the intricacies of decision-making processes allows leaders and managers to navigate complexities, address challenges effectively, and capitalize on opportunities.

Let's look into the multifaceted world of organizational decision-making by exploring several influential theories and models that offer diverse perspectives on how decisions are formulated within organizations.

We begin with the Behavioral Theory of the Firm, developed by Richard Cyert and James March. This theory challenges traditional economic models that view firms as rational, profit-maximizing entities. Instead, it presents a more realistic depiction of organizations as coalitions of individuals and groups with varying goals and limited rationality. By highlighting the processes of satisficing, problemistic search, and organizational learning, Cyert and March provide a nuanced understanding of how real-world decisions are made within firms.

Next, we examine the Garbage Can Model of Organizational Choice, which offers a starkly different view of decision-making. Developed by Michael Cohen, James March, and Johan Olsen, this model suggests that decision-making in organizations can often be chaotic and unstructured. It posits that decisions result from the random confluence of problems, solutions, participants, and choice opportunities, highlighting the inherent unpredictability and fluidity of organizational life.

The chapter also explores the role of political language and symbols in decision-making. This perspective underscores the power of rhetoric, imagery, and symbolic actions in shaping organizational choices. Political language and symbols can influence perceptions, legitimize decisions, and mobilize support, playing a crucial role in how decisions are communicated and enacted within organizations.

Through these theories and models, we aim to provide a comprehensive understanding of the complex and often messy reality of decision-making in organizations. By integrating insights from behavioral theory, the garbage can model, and the study of political language, this chapter equips you with the knowledge to navigate and influence decision-making processes effectively.

As you explore these concepts, consider how they apply to your organizational context and how you can leverage them to enhance decision-making in your business. Whether you are striving to improve strategic planning, manage change, or lead your team more effectively, the insights from this chapter will help you understand the dynamics of decision-making and develop strategies to make better, more informed choices.

Behavioral Theory of the Firm (Cyert and March)

The Behavioral Theory of the Firm, developed by Richard Cyert and James March in their seminal work in the early 1960s, offers a groundbreaking perspective on how organizations make decisions. Departing from traditional economic theories that view firms as rational entities focused solely on profit maximization, Cyert and March present a more realistic and complex view of organizational behavior.

At the heart of the Behavioral Theory of the Firm is the recognition that organizations are coalitions of individuals and groups, each with their own goals, expectations, and perceptions. These coalitions include managers, employees, shareholders, and other stakeholders whose interests often diverge. As a result, organizational decisions emerge from a process of negotiation and compromise among these various parties, rather than from a single, unified pursuit of profit.

A central concept in Cyert and March's theory is bounded rationality. This concept acknowledges that individuals within organizations operate under significant constraints, including limited information, cognitive limitations, and the influence of organizational norms and routines. Unlike the traditional notion of perfect rationality, bounded rationality suggests that decision-makers aim for satisfactory solutions rather than optimal ones—a concept known as satisficing.

The theory also highlights that organizational goals are not fixed; instead, they evolve through continuous negotiation processes among coalition members. Different groups within the organization, such as departments or teams, have distinct objectives—such as growth, stability, or innovation—that can conflict with one another. The overall goals of the organization are thus a compromise that balances these competing interests.

Cyert and March identify several key behavioral processes that influence organizational decision-making:

- Problemistic Search: Organizations typically engage in problem-driven searches when they encounter issues or performance gaps. This search process is often localized and focused on finding solutions that are close at hand, building on existing practices and knowledge.

- Organizational Learning: Firms learn from their past experiences and actions, which shapes future decisions. This learning is incremental and path-dependent, meaning that historical choices and established routines significantly influence the organization's current behavior and strategies.

- Standard Operating Procedures: Organizations develop routines and standard operating procedures to manage complexity and ensure consistency in their operations. These routines guide decision-making and behavior, reducing uncertainty and facilitating coordination among members.

- Coalition Formation: The decision-making process involves forming coalitions among different groups within the organization. These coalitions negotiate and influence the firm's goals, resource allocation, and strategic directions, reflecting the diverse interests and power dynamics at play.

Consider a hypothetical example of TechWave, a mid-sized technology firm facing competitive pressures. TechWave's management team, employees, and shareholders each have different priorities. Shareholders demand higher profitability, managers focus on long-term growth, and employees seek innovation and job security. When TechWave encounters a decline in market share, it engages in problemistic search, exploring potential solutions such as entering new markets or enhancing product features. The search is influenced by past experiences and the firm's established routines, such as its reliance on specific technologies.

The decision-making process at TechWave involves negotiations among different coalitions. Management pushes for strategic investments in new technology, while the R&D team advocates for increased funding for innovation. The resulting decision—a compromise solution that balances immediate financial performance with long-term growth and innovation goals—reflects bounded rationality. It is not the optimal solution for any single group but a satisfactory outcome for the organization as a whole.

The Behavioral Theory of the Firm provides a realistic framework for understanding the complexities of organizational decision-making. It highlights the importance of internal negotiations, the constraints of bounded rationality, and the role of routines and learning in shaping behavior. By recognizing that firms operate as coalitions of diverse stakeholders with evolving goals, this theory offers valuable insights into the adaptive and dynamic nature of organizations.

For managers and leaders, understanding these processes can enhance their ability to navigate complex decision-making environments. It encourages a more nuanced approach that considers the varied interests and limitations of different organizational members, fostering better strategies and more cohesive outcomes. By applying the principles of the Behavioral Theory of the Firm, organizations can improve their decision-making processes, align their goals more effectively, and enhance their overall adaptability and resilience in a rapidly changing business landscape.

Garbage Can Model of Organizational Choice

The Garbage Can Model of Organizational Choice, developed by Michael Cohen, James March, and Johan Olsen in the early 1970s, offers a distinctive and illuminating perspective on decision-making within organizations. This model diverges sharply from traditional approaches that assume decision-making is systematic and rational. Instead, it posits that decision-making in organizations is often chaotic, fluid, and somewhat random.

This model is particularly relevant to what the authors describe as "organized anarchies," which are organizations characterized by problematic preferences, unclear technology, and fluid participation. In such environments, organizational goals are often ambiguous, the processes for achieving these goals are not well understood, and the involvement of participants in decision-making fluctuates over time.

The Garbage Can Model depicts organizational decision-making as a process where four distinct streams flow independently and occasionally intersect: problems, solutions, participants, and choice opportunities. These streams come together in a metaphorical "garbage can," where decisions are made when the right combination of these elements happens to converge.

Problems represent the issues or concerns that need to be addressed. These can arise from various internal or external sources and can vary in urgency and importance. Solutions are the ideas or answers that may solve problems. These solutions often exist independently of the problems and may be proposed even when there is no immediate issue to address. Participants are the individuals involved in the decision-making process. Their level of involvement and interest can fluctuate based on other commitments and personal agendas. Choice opportunities are the moments or situations when decisions need to be made, such as meetings, deadlines, or crises.

In the Garbage Can Model, decision-making is less about rational planning and more about the coincidental alignment of these streams. Decisions occur when the right problems, solutions, participants, and choice opportunities converge in the same "garbage can."

Consider a hypothetical example of Innovatech, a tech startup experiencing rapid growth and facing numerous challenges. Innovatech operates in a highly dynamic environment where priorities shift frequently, and participation in decision-making varies among its team members. One day, Innovatech's product development team is grappling with a significant technical problem that has stalled a critical project. At the same time, a solution in the form of a new software tool is proposed by a team member who has been exploring innovative technologies. However, this solution does not initially gain much attention because the team's focus is scattered across various issues.

Coincidentally, the company's CEO announces an impromptu meeting to address an unrelated operational issue. This meeting brings together key participants who have been working on different aspects of the project. During the discussion, the technical problem is brought up, and the proposed software tool is reintroduced. The convergence of the problem (technical issue), solution (new software tool), participants (key team members), and choice opportunity (the impromptu meeting) leads to a decision to implement the software tool to resolve the technical issue. In this scenario, the decision was not the result of a linear, rational process but rather the coincidental alignment of the four streams within the "garbage can." This example illustrates how decisions in organizations can emerge from seemingly haphazard and unplanned interactions.

The Garbage Can Model underscores the importance of understanding the fluid and often chaotic nature of decision-making in organizations, especially in environments characterized by ambiguity and rapid change. It challenges the assumption that decisions are always the product of deliberate and systematic processes. Instead, it highlights how decision-making can be influenced by timing, context, and the coincidental alignment of different elements.

For managers and leaders, the Garbage Can Model offers several practical insights. It highlights the need to create environments where spontaneous and informal interactions can occur, as these can lead to unexpected but valuable decision-making opportunities. Managers should be aware of the timing and context in which problems, solutions, participants, and choice opportunities converge, as this can significantly influence the outcomes of decisions. Flexibility and adaptability are also crucial, recognizing that decision-making processes may not always follow predictable patterns. By fostering a culture that embraces the unpredictability of decision-making and leveraging it for innovative and adaptive solutions, organizations can better navigate complex and dynamic environments.

The Garbage Can Model of Organizational Choice provides a compelling and unconventional framework for understanding decision-making in organizations. By acknowledging the inherent chaos and fluidity of organizational life, this model offers valuable insights into how decisions can emerge from the interplay of various independent streams. Managers and leaders can use these insights to navigate complex environments more effectively, fostering a culture that embraces the unpredictability of decision-making and leverages it for innovative and adaptive solutions.

Political Language and Symbols

In organizational settings, political language and symbols play a crucial role in shaping perceptions, influencing behavior, and facilitating decision-making processes. Political language refers to the strategic use of rhetoric, narratives, and framing to guide and control the interpretation of events and decisions. Symbols, on the other hand, encompass a wide range of elements such as gestures, rituals, artifacts, and visual imagery that convey deeper meanings and values within the organization. Together, these tools are powerful in navigating the complex and often ambiguous landscape of organizational politics.

Political language is employed by leaders and other influential figures within an organization to frame issues, set agendas, and mobilize support. By carefully crafting messages, leaders can align organizational members with their vision and strategic goals. For example, a CEO might use inspirational language to rally employees around a new strategic initiative, emphasizing themes of innovation, progress, and shared purpose. This rhetorical approach not only clarifies the goals but also motivates and engages employees, creating a sense of unity and commitment.

The framing of issues is another essential aspect of political language. By presenting problems and solutions in a specific way, leaders can shape how these issues are perceived and understood by organizational members. For instance, a manager might frame a budget cut as an opportunity for increased efficiency and innovation rather than a mere reduction in resources. This positive framing can help mitigate resistance and foster a more constructive response from employees.

Symbols, as non-verbal tools of communication, carry significant weight in reinforcing organizational culture and values. They can manifest in various forms, including logos, slogans, office layouts, ceremonies, and even dress codes. These symbols help create a shared identity and convey the underlying principles that guide organizational behavior. For example, an open office layout might symbolize transparency and collaboration, while a corporate logo can evoke the organization's history, mission, and aspirations.

Rituals and ceremonies are potent symbolic acts that reinforce organizational values and celebrate achievements. Award ceremonies, annual meetings, and team-building activities are more than just events; they are rituals that strengthen the social fabric of the organization and reaffirm its core values. These ceremonies provide opportunities for leaders to publicly recognize contributions, reinforce desired behaviors, and create a sense of belonging among employees.

Consider a hypothetical example of GlobalHealth, a multinational healthcare organization undergoing a significant transformation to embrace digital health technologies. The CEO of GlobalHealth, aware of the potential resistance to change, employs political language to frame this transformation as a necessary evolution to stay competitive and improve patient care. She uses stories of past successes, highlighting how previous innovations have led to better outcomes, to build a narrative that aligns with the organization's values of excellence and compassion.

In addition to this rhetorical strategy, GlobalHealth introduces symbols to reinforce the message. New digital tools and platforms are branded with a sleek, modern logo that represents innovation and progress. The organization also hosts a series of launch events, where employees are invited to participate in demonstrations of the new technology and hear testimonials from colleagues who have successfully adopted these tools. These events are designed to be celebratory, emphasizing the collective achievement and the exciting future ahead.

Through the strategic use of political language and symbols, the CEO of GlobalHealth successfully navigates the complex landscape of organizational change. Employees are not only informed about the transformation but are also emotionally and symbolically connected to the new direction of the organization.

Political language and symbols are indispensable tools for leaders and managers in shaping organizational dynamics. By effectively employing rhetoric, framing, and symbolic actions, leaders can influence perceptions, align behaviors with strategic goals, and foster a cohesive organizational culture. Understanding the power of these tools allows managers to navigate the intricacies of organizational politics more adeptly, creating an environment where strategic initiatives can flourish, and organizational members are engaged and motivated. As you apply these concepts in your own organization, consider how political language and symbols can be harnessed to drive positive change and reinforce the values that underpin your organizational success.

Chapter 6: Power, Politics, and Influence

In any organization, the dynamics of power, politics, and influence are omnipresent and play a crucial role in shaping outcomes, driving change, and achieving goals. Understanding these dynamics is essential for leaders and managers who aim to navigate their organizations effectively and ethically.

Power is the ability to influence the behavior of others and control resources, making it a fundamental aspect of organizational life. It can arise from various sources, including formal authority, expertise, relationships, and access to information. Recognizing the different types of power—legitimate, reward, coercive, expert, referent, and informational—helps leaders understand how to effectively wield influence within their organizations.

Politics, often perceived with a negative connotation, is simply the process through which power is applied and negotiated in organizational settings. Political behavior is inevitable in organizations where resources are limited, goals are diverse, and interests often conflict. Understanding political strategies and tactics enables leaders to navigate these complexities, build coalitions, and effectively advocate for their initiatives.

Influence, the capacity to have an effect on the character, development, or behavior of someone or something, extends beyond formal power. It encompasses the subtle and strategic use of communication, relationships, and behavior to achieve desired outcomes. Leaders who master the art of influence can inspire and mobilize their teams, drive organizational change, and achieve strategic objectives without relying solely on formal authority.

This chapter begins with an exploration of the various sources and types of power within organizations. By examining how power is derived and exercised, we gain insights into the mechanisms that drive organizational behavior and decision-making. Understanding these sources of power helps leaders and managers to leverage their own power effectively and recognize the power dynamics at play in their environments.

Next, we delve into political strategies and tactics, drawing on practical insights and examples to illustrate how leaders can navigate organizational politics. From building alliances and coalitions to understanding the subtleties of organizational culture, these strategies are essential for advancing agendas and achieving goals in complex organizational landscapes. Finally, we address the challenges and opportunities associated with managing organizational politics. Effective management of organizational politics involves recognizing its presence, understanding its impact, and employing ethical and constructive approaches to influence. By fostering a positive political environment, leaders can enhance collaboration, reduce conflict, and drive the organization toward its strategic objectives.

As we explore the intricacies of power, politics, and influence, consider how these dynamics manifest in your own organization and the strategies you can employ to navigate them successfully. Mastering these elements is not only crucial for achieving personal and organizational success but also for creating a work environment where fairness, integrity, and collaboration can thrive.

Sources and Types of Organizational Power

Power within organizations is a fundamental aspect that influences decision-making, behavior, and the overall dynamic of the workplace. Understanding the sources and types of organizational power is crucial for leaders and managers to navigate and wield influence effectively. Power is not monolithic; it derives from various sources and manifests in different forms, each with its own implications and uses.

Legitimate Power

Legitimate power, also known as positional power, stems from an individual's formal position within the organizational hierarchy. This type of power is based on the authority granted by the organization to carry out certain roles and responsibilities. For instance, a CEO, manager, or department head has legitimate power due to their official title and position. Employees are generally expected to comply with the directives of those who hold legitimate power because it is sanctioned by the organization's rules and structure. While legitimate power is essential for maintaining order and coordination, it can be limited if not coupled with other forms of power.

Reward Power

Reward power arises from the ability to distribute rewards that others value, such as bonuses, promotions, raises, or even praise and recognition. This type of power is effective because it directly influences employees' motivation and behavior by offering tangible and intangible benefits. For example, a manager who can allocate desirable projects or provide performance bonuses holds significant reward power. However, the effectiveness of reward power can diminish if rewards are perceived as unfair or if overused, leading to a transactional rather than a transformational relationship.

Coercive Power

Coercive power is the ability to impose penalties or sanctions on others for noncompliance or undesirable behavior. This type of power involves the use of threats or punishment, such as demotions, reprimands, or even termination. While coercive power can be effective in enforcing discipline and compliance, it often has negative side effects, such as resentment, fear, and a decrease in morale. Over-reliance on coercive power can lead to a toxic work environment and high employee turnover.

Expert Power

Expert power derives from an individual's skills, knowledge, and expertise in a particular area. This type of power is based on the perception that the person possesses valuable insights or abilities that are crucial for the organization's success. For instance, a software engineer with deep technical expertise or a financial analyst with a thorough understanding of market trends holds expert power. This power is often more persuasive and enduring because it is rooted in the credibility and respect that others have for the individual's competence. Leaders with expert power can influence others by providing sound advice and demonstrating their expertise in solving complex problems.

Referent Power

Referent power is based on the personal characteristics and relationships of an individual. It arises from the admiration, respect, and loyalty that others have towards them. Charismatic leaders, who inspire and attract followers through their personality, vision, and interpersonal skills, wield referent power. This type of power can be highly effective in motivating and mobilizing people, as it builds strong emotional connections and a sense of loyalty. However, referent power can be difficult to maintain if the leader's actions do not align with the values and expectations of their followers.

Informational Power

Informational power is derived from access to and control over information that is valuable to others. This type of power comes from possessing knowledge that others need to perform their jobs, make decisions, or solve problems. For example, a project manager who has comprehensive information about project timelines, resources, and stakeholders holds informational power. By selectively sharing or withholding information, individuals with informational power can influence the actions and decisions of others. This power is particularly important in environments where information is a critical resource.

Consider a hypothetical example of MedTech Innovations, a healthcare technology company undergoing a major organizational change. The CEO of MedTech, who holds legitimate power, announces a new strategic direction for the company. To implement this change, the CEO relies on various sources and types of power within the organization.

The head of R&D, who possesses expert power due to their extensive knowledge of medical technology, plays a crucial role in convincing the team of the technical feasibility and benefits of the new strategy. The HR director, leveraging reward power, introduces incentive programs to motivate employees to embrace the change and contribute to its success. Meanwhile, the operations manager uses coercive power sparingly to address resistance and ensure compliance with the new processes. Throughout this transition, the CEO also utilizes referent power, building strong personal connections with key stakeholders and communicating a compelling vision that inspires and engages the entire organization. Informational power is managed carefully by the communications director, who ensures that accurate and timely information is disseminated to all employees, reducing uncertainty and fostering a sense of transparency and trust.

Understanding the sources and types of organizational power is essential for effective leadership and management. By recognizing and appropriately leveraging legitimate, reward, coercive, expert, referent, and informational power, leaders can influence behavior, drive change, and achieve organizational goals. Each type of power has its own strengths and limitations, and the most effective leaders are those who can balance and integrate these different sources of power to create a cohesive and dynamic organizational environment.

Political Strategies and Tactics

Navigating the complex landscape of organizational politics requires a deep understanding of various political strategies and tactics. These strategies are essential for leaders and managers who seek to influence decisions, build coalitions, and achieve their objectives within an organization. By effectively employing political strategies and tactics, individuals can leverage their power, manage relationships, and steer their organizations toward success.

One fundamental political strategy is coalition building. Coalitions are alliances of individuals or groups who come together to achieve common goals. In an organizational context, forming coalitions can help leaders garner support for their initiatives, pool resources, and enhance their influence. Building a successful coalition involves identifying potential allies, understanding their interests and motivations, and finding common ground. Effective leaders also know how to maintain these alliances by ensuring that coalition members feel valued and that their contributions are recognized.

Another critical political tactic is the use of networking. Networking involves establishing and nurturing relationships with key individuals both inside and outside the organization. These relationships can provide access to valuable information, resources, and support. Networking requires a genuine interest in others, active listening, and a willingness to offer help and support when needed. By building a strong network, leaders can create a web of connections that can be mobilized to achieve strategic goals.

Influence tactics, such as persuasion and negotiation, are also essential components of political strategy. Persuasion involves convincing others to support a particular course of action by presenting compelling arguments, evidence, and benefits. Effective persuasion requires a clear understanding of the audience's values, needs, and concerns. Negotiation, on the other hand, involves finding mutually acceptable solutions to conflicts or differences. Successful negotiation requires preparation, effective communication, and the ability to find win-win outcomes that satisfy all parties involved.

Managing perceptions is another important political tactic. Leaders must be aware of how they are perceived by others and take steps to shape these perceptions positively. This involves being mindful of one's behavior, communication style, and the signals sent through actions and decisions. By consistently demonstrating competence, integrity, and fairness, leaders can build a positive reputation that enhances their influence and credibility.

Strategic use of information is a powerful political tactic. Information is a critical resource in any organization, and those who control its flow can significantly impact decision-making processes. Leaders must know when and how to share information, ensuring it supports their strategic objectives. This includes timing the release of information, framing it in a way that highlights key points, and ensuring that it reaches the right audience.

Understanding and leveraging the organizational culture is also vital. Every organization has its own set of values, norms, and unwritten rules that influence behavior and decision-making. Effective leaders take the time to understand the organizational culture and use this knowledge to navigate political landscapes. This might involve aligning proposals with cultural values, using culturally resonant symbols and language, and respecting established norms and practices.

Consider a hypothetical example of an ambitious manager, Maria, who aims to implement a new sustainability initiative within her company. To succeed, Maria employs several political strategies and tactics. She begins by building a coalition of like-minded colleagues from different departments, highlighting how the initiative aligns with their interests and the company's strategic goals. Through active networking, she gains the support of key influencers, including senior executives who can champion the initiative. Maria uses persuasion to present a compelling case for the sustainability initiative, backed by data and success stories from other organizations. She also negotiates with departments that might be impacted by the changes, finding ways to address their concerns and secure their buy-in. Throughout the process, Maria is mindful of managing perceptions, consistently demonstrating her commitment to the company's values and the initiative's benefits.

She strategically shares information about the initiative, ensuring that stakeholders receive timely and relevant updates. Maria also leverages the company's culture, framing the initiative in terms of corporate social responsibility, a value deeply ingrained in the organization's ethos. By effectively employing these political strategies and tactics, Maria successfully navigates the organizational landscape, builds broad support for her initiative, and achieves her goal of implementing the sustainability program.

Political strategies and tactics are essential tools for leaders and managers seeking to influence decisions and drive change within their organizations. By building coalitions, networking, persuading, negotiating, managing perceptions, strategically using information, and leveraging organizational culture, leaders can navigate the complexities of organizational politics and achieve their strategic objectives. Understanding and mastering these tactics can significantly enhance a leader's ability to effect positive change and steer their organization toward success.

Managing Organizational Politics

Organizational politics, often perceived negatively, is an inherent aspect of organizational life that, if managed effectively, can be harnessed to drive positive outcomes and foster a healthy work environment. Managing organizational politics involves understanding the underlying dynamics, navigating the complexities of interpersonal relationships, and using strategic approaches to influence decision-making and organizational behavior constructively.

First and foremost, recognizing that politics is a natural part of organizational life is essential. Politics arise from the divergent interests, goals, and power dynamics among individuals and groups within an organization. By accepting this reality, leaders can approach politics not as a problem to be eliminated but as a factor to be managed thoughtfully.

Transparency and communication are crucial in managing organizational politics. Leaders should foster an open and transparent environment where information flows freely and decisions are communicated clearly. Transparency reduces the uncertainty and suspicion that often fuel negative political behavior. Regular updates, open forums for discussion, and clear explanations of decision-making processes help build trust and reduce the likelihood of misinterpretation and rumor-mongering.

Another vital strategy is to promote a culture of inclusiveness and collaboration. Encouraging teamwork and cross-functional collaboration helps break down silos and reduce the competition and rivalry that often lead to destructive political behavior. When individuals and departments work together towards common goals, the emphasis shifts from individual agendas to collective success. This collaborative culture can be fostered through team-building activities, joint projects, and recognizing and rewarding collaborative efforts.

Leaders must also be adept at conflict resolution. Conflicts are inevitable in any organization, but how they are managed can either exacerbate or mitigate political behavior. Leaders should address conflicts promptly and fairly, ensuring that all parties feel heard and understood. Using conflict resolution techniques such as mediation, negotiation, and finding common ground can turn potential political battles into opportunities for growth and improved relationships.

Building strong relationships and networks within the organization is another critical aspect of managing politics. Leaders should invest time in understanding the perspectives, motivations, and concerns of various stakeholders. By developing trust and rapport with key individuals and groups, leaders can create a support base that can be mobilized to influence decisions and drive initiatives. Networking also involves being accessible and approachable, allowing employees to share their insights and concerns openly.

Ethical behavior and integrity are foundational to managing organizational politics effectively. Leaders must model ethical behavior and set clear expectations for conduct within the organization. When leaders act with integrity, they build credibility and trust, which are essential for positive political engagement. Establishing and enforcing a code of ethics helps ensure that political behavior aligns with the organization's values and standards.

Encouraging diversity of thought and perspective can also help manage organizational politics. When leaders create an environment where different viewpoints are valued and considered, it reduces the tendency for political behavior to become divisive. Encouraging open debate and fostering a culture where dissenting opinions can be expressed without fear of retribution helps create more balanced and well-considered decisions.

Consider a hypothetical example of an organization, TechSolutions, that is undergoing a significant restructuring process. The restructuring creates uncertainty and anxiety among employees, leading to an increase in political behavior as individuals and departments vie for influence and resources.

The CEO of TechSolutions recognizes the potential for negative politics and takes proactive steps to manage it. She begins by communicating openly about the reasons for the restructuring, the expected outcomes, and the process involved. Regular updates and Q&A sessions are held to address concerns and keep everyone informed.

To promote collaboration, the CEO establishes cross-functional teams to work on key aspects of the restructuring. These teams include representatives from various departments, ensuring that different perspectives are included in the decision-making process. Team-building activities are organized to strengthen relationships and encourage a spirit of cooperation.

The CEO also focuses on conflict resolution, addressing disputes promptly and fairly. She ensures that conflicts are managed constructively, with an emphasis on finding solutions that are acceptable to all parties involved. This approach helps maintain a positive work environment and reduces the potential for divisive political behavior.

By networking and building strong relationships within the organization, the CEO creates a support base that can be relied upon to influence decisions positively. Her ethical behavior and commitment to transparency build trust and credibility, reinforcing the organization's values and standards.

Through these strategies, the CEO of TechSolutions manages organizational politics effectively, turning a potentially challenging situation into an opportunity for positive change and growth. The restructuring process proceeds smoothly, with broad support and minimal disruption, demonstrating the power of well-managed organizational politics.

Managing organizational politics involves recognizing its inevitability, fostering transparency and communication, promoting collaboration, resolving conflicts constructively, building strong relationships, modeling ethical behavior, and encouraging diversity of thought. By adopting these strategies, leaders can harness the power of politics to drive positive outcomes, create a healthy work environment, and steer their organizations toward success. Understanding and managing organizational politics is not just about avoiding negative behavior but about leveraging political dynamics to achieve strategic objectives and enhance organizational effectiveness.

Understanding and navigating the dynamics of power, politics, and influence is crucial for effective leadership and management within organizations. Recognizing the various sources and types of power, employing strategic political tactics, and managing organizational politics constructively are key components in fostering a productive and positive work environment.

The exploration of power within organizations reveals its multifaceted nature, stemming from legitimate authority, rewards, coercion, expertise, relationships, and control of information. By leveraging these sources of power appropriately, leaders can influence behaviors, drive decisions, and achieve strategic objectives.

Political strategies such as coalition building, networking, and managing perceptions are essential tools for leaders. These strategies help align organizational members with strategic goals, resolve conflicts, and drive initiatives effectively. Managing organizational politics involves promoting transparency, fostering a collaborative culture, resolving conflicts constructively, and building strong relationships based on trust and integrity.

As you reflect on the concepts and examples discussed in this chapter, consider how to apply these insights in your own organizational context. Embrace the inevitability of politics in organizations and view it as an opportunity to influence and drive positive change. Foster a culture of transparency and open communication to build trust and reduce misunderstandings. Encourage collaboration and teamwork to align diverse interests and reduce divisive political behavior. Develop strong conflict resolution skills to address issues promptly and fairly, turning potential conflicts into opportunities for growth. Build and maintain a network of relationships within your organization to enhance your influence and support base. Model ethical behavior and integrity to set a positive example and build credibility. Encourage diversity of thought and open debate to ensure balanced decision-making and innovation.

By mastering the art of managing power, politics, and influence, you can enhance your leadership effectiveness, create a more cohesive and motivated workforce, and achieve your strategic objectives more efficiently. Remember that when managed well, these elements can be powerful forces for good, helping to align efforts, mobilize resources, and drive your organization toward success.

Part IV: Leadership and Culture

Leadership and culture are the twin pillars that shape the identity and success of any organization. Together, they influence everything from strategic direction and operational effectiveness to employee morale and organizational adaptability. In Part IV, we research together these critical elements to understand how they interact and drive organizational excellence.

Leadership is not just about holding a position of authority; it's about influencing and guiding others toward achieving common goals. Over the years, leadership theories have evolved from traditional models that emphasize hierarchical control to contemporary approaches that value collaboration, innovation, and adaptability. We will explore these theories, examining how they have shifted to meet the demands of an ever-changing business landscape. The capacity for collaborative leadership and the importance of prior partnerships in achieving organizational success will be highlighted, particularly in the context of accountable care organizations (ACO) and accountable health communities (ACH), where executive leadership plays a pivotal role in navigating complex health ecosystems.

Organizational culture and climate, while often used interchangeably, have distinct meanings and impacts on the organization. Culture refers to the shared values, beliefs, and norms that influence how people behave within an organization, while climate is the perception of these values and norms, reflected in the work environment and employee interactions. A strong, positive culture can drive high performance, foster innovation, and facilitate change, whereas a negative culture can impede progress and lead to disengagement.

In this section, we will define and differentiate between culture and climate, exploring their profound impact on organizational performance and change initiatives. We will also delve into the crucial role of trust at various levels within the organization, examining how it affects relationships, decision-making, and overall organizational health. Trust is the glue that holds the social fabric of an organization together, and understanding its nuances and impacts can help leaders foster a more cohesive and resilient organization.

As you embark on this journey through leadership and culture, consider how these concepts apply to your own organization. Reflect on the leadership practices that have shaped your experience and the cultural elements that define your workplace. This exploration will equip you with insights and tools to enhance your leadership capabilities and cultivate a thriving organizational culture, driving sustainable success in an increasingly complex and dynamic world.

Chapter 7: Leadership Theories and Practices

Leadership is a cornerstone of organizational success, guiding vision, shaping culture, and driving performance. We now explore the rich tapestry of leadership theories and practices, examining how they have evolved over time and their implications for modern organizations.

We begin by contrasting traditional and contemporary leadership theories. Traditional leadership theories, such as the Great Man Theory and Trait Theory, emphasize inherent qualities and characteristics believed to distinguish leaders from non-leaders. These theories often focus on hierarchical structures, with leadership seen as a top-down process driven by authority and control. However, as organizations and their environments have become more complex and dynamic, contemporary leadership theories have emerged to address these changes. Theories such as Transformational Leadership, Servant Leadership, and Adaptive Leadership emphasize the importance of vision, collaboration, and the ability to navigate and drive change within fluid and often uncertain contexts. These modern approaches highlight the relational and dynamic aspects of leadership, focusing on how leaders can inspire, empower, and engage their followers to achieve collective goals.

Next, we explore the concept of collaborative capacity and the significance of prior partnerships in enhancing organizational leadership. In today's interconnected and interdependent world, the ability to collaborate effectively is crucial for organizational success. Collaborative capacity refers to an organization's ability to work effectively across boundaries, whether they are departmental, organizational, or sectoral. Leaders who can cultivate and leverage partnerships, both internal and external, can enhance their organization's innovation, adaptability, and overall performance. Prior successful partnerships build trust and provide a foundation for future collaboration, making it easier to mobilize resources, share knowledge, and achieve common goals.

The role of executive leadership in organizations is another critical focus of this chapter. Executive leaders, such as CEOs and senior managers, play a pivotal role in shaping the strategic direction and overall health of their organizations. They are responsible for setting the vision, establishing goals, and creating an environment that fosters high performance and engagement. Effective executive leadership involves balancing strategic foresight with operational execution, navigating complex stakeholder relationships, and driving organizational change. In particular, the chapter will examine the role of executive leadership within specific contexts such as Accountable Care Organizations (ACOs) and Accountable Health Communities (ACHs), where leaders must navigate complex, multi-stakeholder environments to improve health outcomes and organizational efficiency.

As we explore these themes, consider how they relate to your own experiences and the leadership practices within your organization. Reflect on the evolving nature of leadership and the skills required to lead effectively in today's complex and rapidly changing world. This chapter aims to provide you with a deeper understanding of leadership theories and practices, equipping you with the insights needed to enhance your leadership capabilities and drive your organization toward sustained success.

Traditional vs. Contemporary Leadership Theories

Leadership theories have evolved significantly over time, reflecting changes in organizational needs, societal values, and the complexity of the business environment. Understanding both traditional and contemporary leadership theories provides a comprehensive view of how leadership has been conceptualized and practiced throughout history.

Traditional Leadership Theories

Traditional leadership theories often emphasize the inherent qualities and characteristics that distinguish leaders from non-leaders. These theories typically focus on top-down leadership, where authority and control are centralized.

One of the earliest traditional theories is the Great Man Theory, which posits that leaders are born, not made. This theory suggests that great leaders possess inherent traits and qualities that predispose them to leadership. Historical figures like Alexander the Great and Winston Churchill are often cited as examples of this theory, which implies that leadership cannot be taught or developed; it is an innate characteristic.

Closely related to the Great Man Theory is the Trait Theory, which identifies specific traits that are common among successful leaders. Traits such as intelligence, confidence, charisma, and decisiveness are considered essential for effective leadership. While Trait Theory provides valuable insights into the attributes of leaders, it has been criticized for its lack of consideration for context and situational factors that influence leadership effectiveness.

The Behavioral Theory of leadership emerged as a response to the limitations of trait-based approaches. Instead of focusing on inherent traits, Behavioral Theory examines the behaviors and actions of leaders. This theory posits that effective leadership can be learned and developed through the adoption of certain behaviors. Key behavioral approaches include the Michigan Leadership Studies and the Ohio State Leadership Studies, which identify task-oriented and people-oriented behaviors as critical components of leadership.

Contingency Theories introduced the idea that the effectiveness of leadership depends on the interaction between the leader's traits or behaviors and the situational context. The Fiedler Contingency Model, for example, suggests that the effectiveness of a leader is contingent upon the match between the leader's style and the demands of the situation. This theory highlights the importance of context in determining leadership effectiveness and suggests that there is no one-size-fits-all approach to leadership.

Contemporary Leadership Theories

Contemporary leadership theories reflect a shift towards understanding the relational and dynamic aspects of leadership, emphasizing adaptability, collaboration, and the ability to inspire and engage followers.

Transformational Leadership is one of the most influential contemporary theories. Transformational leaders are characterized by their ability to inspire and motivate followers to achieve higher levels of performance and to embrace change. These leaders focus on vision, communication, and fostering an environment of trust and collaboration. Transformational leaders are often seen as change agents who can guide their organizations through periods of significant transformation.

Servant Leadership is another contemporary approach that emphasizes the leader's role as a servant to their followers. This theory, popularized by Robert Greenleaf, suggests that effective leaders prioritize the needs of their followers, empower them, and help them develop and perform at their best. Servant leaders focus on empathy, listening, and stewardship, fostering a supportive and inclusive organizational culture.

Adaptive Leadership highlights the ability of leaders to navigate complex and rapidly changing environments. This approach, developed by Ronald Heifetz, emphasizes the importance of flexibility, learning, and the ability to address adaptive challenges that do not have clear solutions. Adaptive leaders engage with their followers to identify challenges, experiment with new approaches, and learn from failures.

Situational Leadership, developed by Paul Hersey and Ken Blanchard, builds on the contingency approach by suggesting that leaders should adjust their style based on the maturity and competence of their followers. This theory identifies four leadership styles—directing, coaching, supporting, and delegating—and posits that effective leaders are those who can adapt their approach to meet the needs of their team members.

Collaborative Leadership focuses on the ability to lead through influence rather than authority, emphasizing the importance of building relationships, fostering collaboration, and creating networks of trust. This approach is particularly relevant in today's interconnected and interdependent organizational environments, where leaders must often work across boundaries to achieve common goals.

Distributed Leadership is another contemporary theory that recognizes the distributed nature of leadership across various levels of the organization. This approach suggests that leadership is not confined to those in formal positions of authority but can be exercised by individuals throughout the organization. Distributed leadership encourages a more democratic and inclusive approach to decision-making and problem-solving.

While traditional leadership theories provide valuable insights into the traits and behaviors associated with effective leadership, contemporary theories offer a more nuanced understanding of the relational, adaptive, and collaborative aspects of leadership. By integrating the strengths of both traditional and contemporary approaches, leaders can develop a more comprehensive and flexible leadership style that is responsive to the complexities of the modern organizational landscape. As you reflect on these theories, consider how they apply to your own leadership experiences and how you can incorporate these insights to enhance your effectiveness as a leader.

Collaborative Capacity and Prior Partnerships

In today's interconnected and interdependent organizational landscape, the ability to collaborate effectively is a critical determinant of success. Collaborative capacity refers to an organization's ability to work seamlessly across internal and external boundaries, leveraging the strengths and resources of diverse stakeholders to achieve common goals. Building and maintaining this capacity often hinges on the organization's history of prior partnerships and its ability to foster trust, communication, and mutual benefit among collaborators.

Understanding Collaborative Capacity

Collaborative capacity involves several key components, including the skills and abilities of individuals within the organization, the processes and structures that facilitate collaboration, and the cultural norms that support cooperative behavior. Organizations with high collaborative capacity can quickly and efficiently mobilize resources, share knowledge, and coordinate actions across different groups, both within the organization and with external partners.

Effective collaboration requires certain competencies among team members, such as communication, conflict resolution, and problem-solving skills. Additionally, it requires leaders who can cultivate an environment that encourages teamwork, respects diverse perspectives, and promotes the free flow of information. Organizations must also establish clear processes and structures, such as cross-functional teams, regular interdepartmental meetings, and collaborative platforms, to facilitate cooperation.

The Role of Prior Partnerships

Prior partnerships play a crucial role in enhancing collaborative capacity. When organizations have a history of successful collaborations, they build a foundation of trust, mutual understanding, and effective communication. These past experiences create a track record that can be leveraged in future partnerships, making it easier to establish new collaborative relationships and enhance existing ones.

For example, an organization that has previously worked with various suppliers on joint product development projects will have developed trust and mutual respect with those partners. This history can expedite the negotiation and implementation of new projects, as both parties are familiar with each other's capabilities, expectations, and working styles. Prior partnerships also provide valuable insights into what strategies and practices work best, allowing the organization to refine its collaborative approaches continuously.

Building Collaborative Capacity

Building collaborative capacity involves deliberate efforts to cultivate the skills, processes, and cultural norms that support effective collaboration. This starts with leadership commitment to fostering a collaborative culture. Leaders must model collaborative behavior, such as actively seeking input from others, demonstrating openness to different perspectives, and valuing teamwork over individual achievement.

Training and development programs can enhance the collaborative skills of employees, equipping them with the tools they need to communicate effectively, manage conflicts constructively, and work cohesively in teams. Organizations should also invest in collaborative technologies and platforms that facilitate real-time communication, information sharing, and project management across different groups.

Creating opportunities for informal interactions and relationship-building is another important aspect of enhancing collaborative capacity. Social events, team-building activities, and informal gatherings can help build trust and camaraderie among team members, laying the groundwork for more effective formal collaborations.

Leveraging Prior Partnerships

To leverage prior partnerships effectively, organizations should document and analyze past collaborative efforts to identify best practices and lessons learned. This institutional knowledge can be used to inform future collaborations, ensuring that successful strategies are replicated and potential pitfalls are avoided.

Organizations should also maintain regular communication with past partners, even when not actively collaborating on projects. This ongoing engagement helps keep relationships strong and positions the organization as a reliable and trusted partner. When new opportunities for collaboration arise, these established relationships can be quickly mobilized.

Consider a hypothetical example of MedTech Innovations, a healthcare technology company with a strong track record of collaborating with hospitals, universities, and research institutions. Over the years, MedTech has successfully developed several innovative medical devices through these partnerships, building a reputation for reliability and innovation.

MedTech's collaborative capacity is enhanced by its prior partnerships. The company has established processes for joint research and development, clear communication channels, and a culture that values teamwork and external collaboration. When a new opportunity arises to develop a cutting-edge diagnostic tool, MedTech quickly mobilizes its network of partners. The existing trust and mutual understanding expedite the negotiation process and facilitate the seamless integration of efforts across different organizations.

By leveraging its collaborative capacity and prior partnerships, MedTech is able to bring the new diagnostic tool to market faster and more efficiently than its competitors. The successful collaboration not only strengthens existing relationships but also enhances MedTech's reputation, attracting new potential partners and opportunities for future collaboration.

Collaborative capacity and prior partnerships are critical assets for any organization seeking to thrive in today's complex and dynamic business environment. By investing in the skills, processes, and cultural norms that support effective collaboration, and by leveraging the trust and mutual understanding built through prior partnerships, organizations can enhance their ability to achieve strategic goals, innovate, and adapt to changing conditions. As you consider your own organization's collaborative efforts, think about how you can build and sustain collaborative capacity and how you can leverage past partnerships to drive future success.

The Role of Executive Leadership in ACO/ACH Organizations

Executive leadership plays a pivotal role in the success of Accountable Care Organizations (ACOs) and Accountable Health Communities (ACHs). These organizations operate within complex and dynamic environments, requiring strong leadership to navigate the multifaceted challenges they face. Executive leaders in ACOs and ACHs are responsible for setting strategic direction, fostering collaboration, ensuring high-quality care, and driving innovation to improve health outcomes and operational efficiency.

Strategic Direction and Vision

One of the primary responsibilities of executive leaders in ACOs and ACHs is to establish a clear strategic direction and vision. This involves setting long-term goals that align with the mission of providing high-quality, patient-centered care while controlling costs. Executives must articulate a compelling vision that inspires and engages all stakeholders, including healthcare providers, patients, payers, and community organizations. This vision serves as a guiding star for all initiatives and decisions, ensuring that the organization remains focused on its core objectives.

Fostering Collaboration and Integration

ACOs and ACHs thrive on collaboration and integration across various healthcare entities. Executive leaders are instrumental in fostering a culture of teamwork and cooperation among diverse stakeholders. This includes building and maintaining strong relationships with physicians, hospitals, community health providers, and social service organizations. By promoting a collaborative environment, executives can facilitate the sharing of information and resources, leading to more coordinated and comprehensive care for patients.

Effective leaders in ACOs and ACHs also champion the integration of services across the continuum of care. This involves breaking down silos between different healthcare providers and ensuring seamless transitions for patients as they move from primary care to specialty care, hospital care, and community services. Executives must advocate for and implement integrated care models that improve care coordination and patient outcomes.

Ensuring Quality and Accountability

Quality care is a cornerstone of ACOs and ACHs, and executive leaders play a critical role in establishing and maintaining high standards of care. They are responsible for implementing robust quality improvement programs and monitoring performance metrics to ensure that care delivery meets or exceeds established benchmarks. This includes setting up systems for data collection and analysis, which are essential for tracking progress and identifying areas for improvement.

Executives must also foster a culture of accountability within the organization. This involves creating clear expectations for performance, providing ongoing education and training for healthcare providers, and establishing mechanisms for feedback and accountability. By holding all stakeholders accountable for their roles in delivering high-quality care, executive leaders can drive continuous improvement and ensure that the organization meets its quality and performance goals.

Driving Innovation and Adaptability

The healthcare landscape is continually evolving, and ACOs and ACHs must be able to adapt to new challenges and opportunities. Executive leaders are tasked with driving innovation within their organizations, encouraging the adoption of new technologies, care models, and best practices. This includes exploring innovative approaches to care delivery, such as telehealth, data analytics, and population health management strategies.

Leaders must also be adept at navigating regulatory changes and shifting reimbursement models. This requires staying informed about policy developments and advocating for regulatory frameworks that support the goals of ACOs and ACHs. By being proactive and adaptable, executives can position their organizations to thrive in a rapidly changing environment.

Engaging Patients and Communities

Patient and community engagement are vital components of ACOs and ACHs, as these organizations aim to address the social determinants of health and improve population health outcomes. Executive leaders must prioritize strategies to engage patients in their own care, promote preventive health measures, and involve community organizations in health initiatives.

This involves implementing patient-centered care practices that empower individuals to take an active role in managing their health. Executives should also work to build partnerships with community organizations that provide essential services such as housing, nutrition, and transportation, which can significantly impact health outcomes. By fostering strong community ties and addressing broader social determinants, executive leaders can enhance the overall well-being of the populations they serve.

The role of executive leadership in ACOs and ACHs is multifaceted and critical to the success of these organizations. Executives must set a clear strategic vision, foster collaboration and integration, ensure quality and accountability, drive innovation, and engage patients and communities. Their leadership is essential in navigating the complexities of the healthcare environment and achieving the goals of improved health outcomes, better patient experiences, and cost-effective care. As healthcare continues to evolve, the importance of strong, visionary, and adaptable executive leadership in ACOs and ACHs will only grow, ensuring that these organizations can meet the needs of their patients and communities effectively.

In this chapter, we explored various leadership theories and practices, highlighting the evolution from traditional to contemporary approaches and their relevance in today's complex organizational environments. Traditional leadership theories, such as the Great Man Theory and Trait Theory, emphasized inherent qualities and hierarchical control. In contrast, contemporary theories like Transformational Leadership, Servant Leadership, and Adaptive Leadership focus on vision, collaboration, and adaptability, reflecting the dynamic nature of modern organizations.

We examined the concept of collaborative capacity and the significance of prior partnerships in enhancing organizational leadership. Effective collaboration, grounded in trust and mutual understanding built through successful past partnerships, enables organizations to mobilize resources, share knowledge, and coordinate actions efficiently.

The role of executive leadership in ACOs and ACHs was also discussed, emphasizing the need for strategic vision, fostering collaboration, ensuring quality and accountability, driving innovation, and engaging with patients and communities. Executive leaders in these complex healthcare environments must navigate multifaceted challenges and adapt to changing conditions to achieve high-quality, cost-effective care.

While this chapter provided an overview of key leadership theories and practices, it merely scratches the surface of this vast and multifaceted field. Leadership is an ever-evolving discipline, shaped by ongoing research, changing organizational contexts, and emerging global trends. As we continue to explore leadership and its impact on organizational success, it is crucial to remain open to new ideas, adaptable in our approaches, and committed to continuous learning and development.

Upcoming are the intricacies of organizational culture and climate, examining how these elements influence performance, change, and trust within organizations. Understanding the interplay between leadership and culture will further enhance our ability to foster environments where individuals and organizations can thrive.

Chapter 8: Organizational Culture and Climate

Organizational culture and climate are two critical aspects that profoundly shape the experiences, behaviors, and performance of individuals within any organization. While these concepts are often used interchangeably, they represent distinct elements of the workplace environment that together influence the overall effectiveness and health of an organization.

Organizational culture refers to the shared values, beliefs, norms, and practices that characterize an organization. It encompasses the unwritten rules and collective behaviors that guide how people interact, make decisions, and approach their work. Culture is deeply embedded in the fabric of the organization, influencing everything from leadership styles and communication patterns to conflict resolution and innovation. Understanding and shaping organizational culture is crucial for leaders who aim to align the workforce with the organization's strategic vision and goals.

In contrast, organizational climate is the perceptual and experiential aspect of the work environment. It reflects employees' collective perceptions and attitudes about their workplace, including their views on leadership, policies, procedures, and interpersonal relationships. Climate can be thought of as the "mood" or "feel" of the organization at a given time, which can fluctuate based on internal and external factors. A positive climate fosters engagement, motivation, and satisfaction, whereas a negative climate can lead to disengagement and high turnover.

The interplay between organizational culture and climate significantly impacts performance and the ability to manage change. A strong, positive culture that aligns with organizational goals can drive high performance, foster innovation, and enhance employee satisfaction. Conversely, a misaligned or toxic culture can impede progress, reduce morale, and increase resistance to change.

Climate acts as a barometer of the organizational environment, providing insights into how employees are likely to respond to new initiatives and changes. Leaders who understand the climate can better anticipate challenges, address concerns, and implement strategies that promote a supportive and productive work environment. Managing the climate effectively during times of change is crucial for minimizing disruption and achieving successful outcomes.

Trust in Organizations

Trust is a foundational element that underpins both culture and climate. It operates at various levels within an organization, from interpersonal trust between colleagues to institutional trust in leadership and organizational systems. High levels of trust facilitate open communication, collaboration, and a willingness to take risks, all of which are essential for innovation and adaptability. Conversely, a lack of trust can lead to skepticism, conflict, and disengagement.

Building and maintaining trust requires consistent actions and behaviors that demonstrate reliability, integrity, and fairness. Leaders play a pivotal role in fostering trust by setting the tone at the top, modeling ethical behavior, and creating transparent and inclusive processes. Trust is not only crucial for day-to-day operations but also becomes especially important during periods of change, where it can significantly influence how employees perceive and respond to new strategies and initiatives.

Let's now explore the definitions and distinctions of organizational culture and climate, exploring their profound impact on performance and change management. We will examine the various levels and impacts of trust within organizations, highlighting strategies for building and sustaining trust. By understanding these elements, leaders can create environments that support high performance, adaptability, and long-term success.

As we explore these concepts, reflect on the culture and climate of your own organization and consider how they influence your work experience and effectiveness. This understanding will equip you with the insights needed to foster a positive environment that aligns with your strategic goals and supports the well-being and engagement of all members of your organization.

Going Deeper with Culture and Climate

Understanding and defining organizational culture and climate is essential for leaders aiming to cultivate a productive and positive work environment. While closely related, culture and climate are distinct concepts that together shape the workplace experience. Here, we delve deeper into these concepts, providing practical advice and examples to help leaders effectively define and influence them.

Organizational culture is the shared values, beliefs, norms, and practices that characterize an organization. It is the invisible yet powerful force that influences behavior, decision-making, and interactions within the organization. To define and understand your organizational culture, consider the following practical steps:

1. Assess Current Culture: Conduct surveys, focus groups, and interviews to gather insights into the existing culture. Ask employees about their perceptions, values, and experiences. Use tools like the Organizational Culture Assessment Instrument (OCAI) to identify dominant cultural attributes.

2. Identify Core Values and Beliefs: Determine the fundamental values and beliefs that underpin your organization. These might include innovation, customer focus, teamwork, integrity, and accountability. Engage leadership and employees in discussions to articulate these core values clearly.

3. Examine Symbols and Artifacts: Observe the physical and symbolic elements of the workplace, such as office layout, dress code, and company rituals. These artifacts reflect and reinforce the underlying culture. For instance, an open office layout might symbolize transparency and collaboration, while regular team-building activities can emphasize the importance of teamwork.

4. Analyze Leadership Styles: Leadership behavior significantly shapes organizational culture. Reflect on how leaders interact with employees, make decisions, and communicate. Leaders who model desired cultural attributes, such as openness and inclusivity, help reinforce those values across the organization.

5. Review Policies and Practices: Evaluate organizational policies, procedures, and practices to ensure they align with the desired culture. For example, performance appraisal systems should reflect and reward behaviors that support core values.

At TechStartup, a company that prides itself on innovation and agility, the leadership team conducted a comprehensive cultural assessment. They discovered that while innovation was a stated value, employees felt constrained by bureaucratic processes. To realign the culture, leaders introduced more flexible work arrangements, reduced approval layers for new projects, and celebrated innovative ideas through regular "innovation showcases." By aligning policies and leadership behaviors with their core value of innovation, TechStartup fostered a culture that genuinely supports creativity and agility.

Organizational climate refers to employees' collective perceptions of their work environment. It reflects the mood or feel of the organization and can vary over time. To define and enhance your organizational climate, consider these practical steps:

1. Measure Employee Perceptions: Use climate surveys to gather data on employee perceptions of the work environment. Focus

on aspects such as job satisfaction, trust in leadership, communication effectiveness, and the sense of support and recognition.

2. Identify Strengths and Areas for Improvement: Analyze survey results to identify positive aspects of the climate and areas needing improvement. Pay attention to trends and patterns that indicate underlying issues.

3. Promote Open Communication: Foster an environment where employees feel comfortable sharing their thoughts and feedback. Regular town hall meetings, suggestion boxes, and anonymous feedback channels can help leaders stay attuned to the organizational climate.

4. Enhance Recognition and Support: Ensure that employees feel valued and supported. Implement recognition programs that celebrate achievements and contributions. Provide opportunities for professional development and growth to show that the organization invests in its people.

5. Monitor and Adjust: Climate can change rapidly, so it's important to monitor it continuously. Conduct regular check-ins and follow-up surveys to track progress and make necessary adjustments.

HealthCareCo, a large healthcare provider, noticed through climate surveys that employees felt undervalued and overworked. In response, the executive team launched a comprehensive recognition program, including monthly awards, public acknowledgment of outstanding performance, and personalized thank-you notes from leadership. They also introduced wellness programs to support employees' physical and mental health. These initiatives significantly improved the organizational climate, leading to higher job satisfaction and lower turnover rates.

While culture is more stable and deeply embedded, climate is more perceptual and can change more quickly. Leaders should strive to align the organizational climate with the desired culture.

This alignment can be achieved by:

- Ensuring that daily interactions and practices reflect core cultural values.

- Using climate assessments as a diagnostic tool to identify misalignments between culture and climate.

- Communicating consistently about cultural values and how they translate into everyday behaviors and decisions.

FinTech Innovations wanted to create a culture of trust and transparency. They found that while their culture emphasized these values, the climate reflected a lack of open communication. To bridge this gap, leaders implemented regular "Ask Me Anything" sessions with the CEO and leadership team, where employees could ask questions and receive candid answers. They also established transparent decision-making processes and shared key business metrics with the entire organization. These actions helped align the climate with the desired culture, fostering a more transparent and trusting work environment.

By understanding and actively managing both organizational culture and climate, leaders can create a cohesive, supportive, and high-performing workplace. This, in turn, enhances employee satisfaction, drives performance, and supports the organization's strategic objectives. As you reflect on these concepts, consider how they apply to your organization and what steps you can take to cultivate a positive culture and climate that align with your goals and values.

Impact on Performance and Change

Organizational culture and climate significantly influence performance and the ability to manage and adapt to change. Understanding this impact is crucial for leaders aiming to foster a productive environment and navigate the complexities of organizational transformations effectively.

Culture's Impact on Performance

Organizational culture, being the bedrock of shared values, beliefs, and norms, profoundly shapes how employees behave and perform. A strong, positive culture aligns employees with the organization's mission and goals, fostering a sense of purpose and commitment. When employees believe in the organizational values and see them reflected in their daily work, they are more likely to exhibit higher levels of engagement, motivation, and productivity. For instance, a culture that values innovation encourages employees to think creatively, take calculated risks, and continuously seek improvement. This can lead to a steady stream of new ideas and improvements in products, services, and processes, driving the organization's competitive edge. Conversely, a culture that is risk-averse and rigid can stifle creativity and innovation, resulting in stagnation and a decline in competitive position.

A culture that emphasizes collaboration and teamwork can enhance performance by fostering a sense of community and support among employees. When collaboration is ingrained in the organizational fabric, employees are more likely to share knowledge, support each other, and work together towards common goals, leading to more efficient problem-solving and higher-quality outcomes.

Climate's Impact on Performance

Organizational climate, which reflects employees' perceptions and attitudes towards their work environment, directly affects their day-to-day experience and performance. A positive climate, characterized by trust, recognition, and open communication, can boost morale and job satisfaction. Employees who feel valued and supported are more likely to be engaged, put in extra effort, and remain loyal to the organization.

For example, a climate that promotes open communication allows employees to express their ideas and concerns without fear of retribution. This can lead to a more innovative and adaptive organization as employees feel empowered to contribute their best ideas and solutions. On the other hand, a climate of fear and mistrust can lead to disengagement, low morale, and high turnover, undermining overall performance.

Culture and Climate's Impact on Change

The ability to manage and adapt to change is increasingly critical in today's fast-paced and complex business environment. Both culture and climate play pivotal roles in an organization's capacity to navigate change effectively.

A strong, adaptive culture is one that values flexibility, learning, and resilience. Such a culture prepares the organization to respond swiftly and effectively to changes in the external environment. Organizations with adaptive cultures are better positioned to embrace change as an opportunity rather than a threat, fostering a proactive rather than reactive approach. Leaders in such cultures encourage experimentation and view failures as learning opportunities, which can significantly enhance the organization's innovation capacity and responsiveness to change.

Climate also impacts how change is perceived and embraced by employees. A positive climate where employees trust leadership and feel secure in their roles can ease the implementation of change initiatives. When employees perceive the work environment as fair, supportive, and transparent, they are more likely to be open to change and less resistant to new initiatives. This acceptance is crucial for the smooth execution of change processes.

Practical Example: Healthcare Transformation

Consider a healthcare organization undergoing a significant transformation to adopt electronic health records (EHR). If the organization's culture strongly supports innovation and continuous improvement, employees are likely to view the transition to EHR as a positive step towards enhancing patient care and operational efficiency. Leaders in this organization would foster an environment that encourages feedback, supports learning, and addresses challenges collaboratively.

The climate, if characterized by trust and open communication, further supports this transition. Employees would feel confident that their concerns about the new system would be heard and addressed. Regular updates and transparent communication from leadership about the benefits and progress of the EHR implementation can reinforce a positive climate, reducing anxiety and resistance among staff.

Managing the Impact on Performance and Change

To leverage culture and climate effectively, leaders must actively shape and manage these elements. This involves continuous assessment and alignment of cultural values and organizational practices with strategic goals. Leaders should foster a positive climate by promoting transparency, recognizing contributions, and providing support and resources for employees to succeed.

During periods of change, it is essential to communicate a clear vision and rationale for the change, align the change initiatives with the core values of the organization, and engage employees throughout the process. By doing so, leaders can mitigate resistance, build trust, and enhance the organization's capacity to adapt and thrive.

Practical Example: Tech Industry Adaptation

In a tech company facing rapid market changes and technological advancements, leaders recognized the need for a cultural shift towards greater agility and innovation. They initiated a series of workshops to redefine the core values, emphasizing flexibility, continuous learning, and customer focus. They also improved the organizational climate by implementing regular town hall meetings where employees could voice their opinions and concerns, creating an open and inclusive communication environment.

As the company introduced new agile methodologies and continuous integration practices, the positive climate and adaptive culture helped employees embrace these changes. The leaders' transparent communication and supportive approach reduced resistance and increased buy-in, enabling the company to swiftly adapt to market demands and maintain its competitive edge.

Organizational culture and climate significantly influence performance and the ability to manage change. Leaders must actively shape and align these elements to foster a productive, innovative, and adaptable organization. By understanding and leveraging the interplay between culture and climate, leaders can drive sustained performance and successfully navigate the complexities of organizational change.

Trust in Organizations

Trust is a foundational element in any organization, influencing everything from employee engagement and collaboration to innovation and overall performance. Trust operates at multiple levels within an organization—interpersonal, team, and organizational—and each level has distinct impacts that collectively contribute to the organization's success.

Interpersonal Trust

Interpersonal trust refers to the trust between individual employees. This type of trust is built through consistent, positive interactions over time and is characterized by confidence in another person's integrity, reliability, and competence. When employees trust one another, they are more likely to share information, collaborate effectively, and support each other's efforts.

For example, in a sales team, interpersonal trust enables members to share leads, offer feedback on sales tactics, and assist each other with challenging clients. This collaborative environment can lead to improved sales performance and a stronger team dynamic.

The absence of interpersonal trust, on the other hand, can lead to silos, reduced communication, and a lack of cooperation. Employees may withhold information, avoid collaboration, and focus solely on their individual goals, which can hinder overall team performance and innovation.

Team Trust

Team trust extends interpersonal trust to the group level. It is the collective confidence that team members have in each other's intentions, capabilities, and commitment to the team's goals. High levels of team trust result in better coordination, more effective problem-solving, and higher levels of creativity and innovation.

Teams with strong trust are more likely to engage in open and honest discussions, take risks, and experiment with new ideas without fear of negative repercussions. This fosters a culture of continuous improvement and learning. For instance, a product development team with high trust will feel comfortable brainstorming bold ideas, providing candid feedback, and iterating quickly based on input from all team members.

Low levels of team trust can lead to dysfunction, characterized by guarded communication, conflict avoidance, and a reluctance to share ideas. This environment stifles innovation and can result in suboptimal solutions to problems.

Organizational Trust

Organizational trust refers to the trust employees have in the organization as a whole, including its leadership, policies, and systems. This type of trust is crucial for employee engagement, morale, and retention. When employees trust their organization, they are more likely to be committed to its goals, motivated to perform well, and willing to go above and beyond in their roles.

High organizational trust is built through transparent communication, consistent and fair practices, and demonstrated integrity by leadership. For example, when leaders communicate openly about the company's direction, involve employees in decision-making processes, and act in accordance with the organization's values, they reinforce trust at the organizational level.

The impacts of organizational trust are far-reaching. Employees who trust their organization are more engaged, exhibit higher job satisfaction, and are less likely to leave the company. They also tend to be more resilient during times of change, as they believe in the organization's ability to navigate challenges effectively.

Conversely, a lack of organizational trust can lead to high turnover, disengagement, and a toxic work environment. Employees may become cynical, disengaged, and unwilling to put in discretionary effort, which can severely impact organizational performance and morale.

Building and Maintaining Trust

Building and maintaining trust at all levels of the organization requires deliberate and ongoing effort. Here are some strategies to foster trust:

- Consistency and Integrity: Leaders and employees alike should act consistently and uphold high ethical standards. This means doing what you say you will do and aligning actions with organizational values.

- Transparent Communication: Open and honest communication is critical. Leaders should share information about the organization's direction, decisions, and challenges. Transparency helps employees feel informed and valued.

- Competence and Reliability: Demonstrating competence in your role and reliability in meeting commitments builds trust. Employees need to see that their colleagues and leaders are capable and dependable.

- Empathy and Support: Showing empathy and providing support to colleagues fosters a trusting environment. This involves understanding others' perspectives, offering help when needed, and recognizing contributions.

- Involvement and Empowerment: Involving employees in decision-making processes and empowering them to take ownership of their work builds trust. When employees feel that their voices are heard and their contributions matter, trust grows.

Practical Example: TechSolutions

Consider TechSolutions, a mid-sized tech company that has recently undergone a major reorganization. To rebuild trust, the CEO initiated a series of town hall meetings where employees could ask questions and receive honest answers about the changes. The leadership team also implemented regular updates on progress and acknowledged mistakes openly.

At the team level, managers were trained to foster open communication and encourage team members to share their ideas and concerns. They instituted regular team-building activities to strengthen interpersonal bonds and built a culture of mutual support and respect.

At the organizational level, TechSolutions revised its performance management system to ensure fairness and transparency, providing clear criteria for evaluations and promotions. They also launched an employee recognition program to celebrate achievements and contributions across all levels of the company.

These efforts led to a significant improvement in trust within TechSolutions. Employees reported feeling more valued and engaged, collaboration across departments increased, and the company saw a boost in overall performance and innovation.

Trust at the interpersonal, team, and organizational levels is essential for a healthy and high-performing organization. By focusing on consistency, transparent communication, competence, empathy, and empowerment, leaders can build and maintain trust, leading to a more engaged, innovative, and resilient workforce. As you reflect on your own organization, consider how these principles can be applied to strengthen trust and enhance overall effectiveness.

In this chapter, we explored the critical concepts of organizational culture and climate, their distinct yet interconnected nature, and their profound impact on performance, change, and trust within organizations. Understanding and effectively managing these elements are essential for fostering a positive work environment and achieving organizational success.

We began by defining organizational culture as the shared values, beliefs, and norms that shape how employees behave and interact within an organization. Culture is deeply ingrained and evolves over time, influencing every aspect of organizational life from decision-making to daily interactions. We emphasized the importance of assessing and actively shaping culture to align with the organization's strategic goals. Practical steps include conducting cultural assessments, identifying core values, examining symbols and artifacts, analyzing leadership styles, and ensuring policies and practices support the desired culture.

Next, we defined organizational climate as the collective perceptions and attitudes of employees toward their work environment. Climate reflects the mood or feel of the organization at a given time and can change more rapidly than culture. We discussed how to measure and improve organizational climate through surveys, promoting open communication, enhancing recognition and support, and regularly monitoring and adjusting based on feedback. A positive climate fosters employee engagement, motivation, and satisfaction, directly impacting performance.

We then examined the interplay between culture and climate and their combined influence on organizational performance and change management. A strong, positive culture aligned with organizational goals drives high performance, fosters innovation, and supports effective change management. Climate acts as a barometer, indicating how employees perceive and react to changes, and is crucial for successful implementation of change initiatives. We provided practical examples to illustrate how leaders can align culture and climate to enhance performance and navigate change effectively.

The chapter also explored the various levels and impacts of trust within organizations—interpersonal, team, and organizational. Trust is the foundation of effective relationships and a critical component of both culture and climate. High levels of trust facilitate open communication, collaboration, and a willingness to take risks, essential for innovation and adaptability. We offered strategies for building and maintaining trust, such as demonstrating consistency and integrity, transparent communication, competence and reliability, empathy and support, and involving and empowering employees.

Organizational culture and climate are powerful forces that shape the work environment and influence overall success. Leaders who understand and actively manage these elements can create a cohesive, supportive, and high-performing organization. By fostering a positive culture and climate, and building trust at all levels, organizations can enhance employee engagement, drive performance, and successfully navigate the complexities of change. As you reflect on the insights and strategies discussed in this chapter, consider how they apply to your own organization and what steps you can take to cultivate a thriving workplace environment that aligns with your strategic goals and supports the well-being of all members.

Part V: Innovation, Change, and Development

In an ever-evolving business landscape, the ability to innovate, adapt, and develop is crucial for organizational success and longevity. Part V of this book focuses on the critical themes of innovation, change, and development, exploring how organizations can foster creativity, implement effective change, and continuously develop to meet new challenges.

Chapter 9 explores innovation and creativity within organizations. We begin by examining various models of innovation, including those proposed by Teresa Amabile and Rosabeth Moss Kanter. Amabile's model highlights the role of individual creativity and intrinsic motivation, while Kanter emphasizes the importance of structural and cultural factors that support innovation. Understanding these models provides a foundation for recognizing and cultivating the conditions necessary for successful innovation.

We will also discuss the key conditions for fostering innovation, such as a supportive culture, open communication, and adequate resources. These conditions create an environment where new ideas can flourish and be effectively implemented. Real-world case studies of organizational innovation will illustrate these concepts, providing tangible examples of how companies have successfully navigated the innovation process.

Chapter 10 shifts the focus to managing change and development within organizations. We will explore various theories of organizational change, including Lewin's Change Management Model and Kotter's 8-Step Process for Leading Change. These theories offer frameworks for understanding how change occurs and how it can be effectively managed.

Strategies for effective change management will be discussed in detail, emphasizing the importance of clear communication, stakeholder engagement, and continuous improvement. These strategies help ensure that change initiatives are successful and sustainable, minimizing resistance and maximizing buy-in from all organizational members. Additionally, we will address the unique challenges faced by organizations in sectors such as healthcare, where change is often complex and multifaceted. By examining specific challenges and strategies for overcoming them, we can gain insights into how to navigate change in highly regulated and rapidly evolving environments.

As we journey through this section, consider how the principles of innovation, change, and development apply to your organization. Reflect on the current state of creativity and adaptability within your workplace and think about the steps you can take to foster a culture that embraces continuous improvement and innovation. This exploration will equip you with the knowledge and tools needed to lead your organization through change and towards sustained development and success.

Chapter 9: Innovation and Creativity in Organizations

Innovation and creativity are the lifeblood of modern organizations, driving growth, competitive advantage, and long-term success. In an era characterized by rapid technological advancements and shifting market demands, organizations must continuously innovate to stay relevant and thrive. Chapter 9 inquire about the critical aspects of fostering innovation and creativity within organizations, offering insights into models of innovation, conditions for success, and real-world examples of innovative practices.

We begin by exploring prominent models of innovation developed by leading scholars Teresa Amabile and Rosabeth Moss Kanter. Amabile's model emphasizes the role of individual creativity, which is influenced by a combination of intrinsic motivation, domain-relevant skills, and creative-thinking skills. According to Amabile, organizational environments that support autonomy, provide resources, and encourage risk-taking can significantly enhance individual creativity, leading to innovative outcomes.

In contrast, Rosabeth Moss Kanter's model of innovation focuses on structural and cultural factors within organizations. Kanter identifies several key elements that contribute to a supportive innovation environment, including diverse teams, open communication channels, and a culture that values experimentation and learning from failure. Kanter's model underscores the importance of leadership in fostering an innovation-friendly climate and creating an organizational structure that facilitates the flow of ideas and collaboration.

Following the exploration of these models, we will discuss the essential conditions for successful innovation. These conditions include a supportive organizational culture, the availability of resources such as time and funding, effective leadership that champions innovation, and processes that encourage experimentation and iterative development. Understanding these conditions helps organizations create an environment where innovation can thrive and be sustained over the long term.

To bring these concepts to life, we will examine case studies of organizations that have successfully implemented innovative practices. These real-world examples will illustrate how different companies have navigated the challenges of fostering innovation, from developing groundbreaking products and services to implementing new business models and processes. By analyzing these case studies, we can identify common themes and best practices that can be applied across various organizational contexts.

As we jump into this chapter, consider how the principles and models of innovation apply to your own organization. Reflect on the current state of creativity within your workplace and think about the steps you can take to enhance your organization's capacity for innovation. This exploration will provide you with valuable insights and practical strategies for fostering a culture of innovation and creativity, enabling your organization to adapt, grow, and succeed in an ever-changing world.

Models of Innovation: Amabile and Kanter

Innovation within organizations is a multifaceted process influenced by individual creativity, organizational structure, and cultural factors. Two prominent models that offer comprehensive insights into fostering innovation are those developed by Teresa Amabile and Rosabeth Moss Kanter. These models provide frameworks for understanding the dynamics of innovation and offer practical strategies for creating environments that support and sustain innovative efforts.

Teresa Amabile's Model of Innovation

Teresa Amabile, a renowned psychologist and professor, has extensively studied the sources of creativity and innovation in organizational settings. Her model emphasizes the interplay between individual creativity and the organizational environment. According to Amabile, creativity is the foundation of innovation and is influenced by three primary components: domain-relevant skills, creativity-relevant skills, and intrinsic motivation.

- Domain-Relevant Skills: These are the knowledge, technical skills, and expertise in a specific field. Employees with strong domain-relevant skills have a deep understanding of their area of work, which enables them to recognize patterns, make connections, and develop innovative solutions.

- Creativity-Relevant Skills: These skills include cognitive abilities, such as divergent thinking, problem-solving, and the ability to think outside the box. Creativity-relevant skills also encompass work habits and personality traits, such as perseverance, openness to new experiences, and a willingness to take risks.

- Intrinsic Motivation: Amabile posits that intrinsic motivation, the drive to engage in activities for their inherent satisfaction and interest, is crucial for creativity. When individuals are intrinsically motivated, they are more likely to experiment, take risks, and persist in the face of challenges, leading to higher levels of creative output.

Amabile's model also highlights the role of the organizational environment in nurturing or hindering creativity. She identifies several environmental factors that can influence individual creativity and, consequently, innovation:

1. Autonomy and Freedom: Providing employees with the autonomy to make decisions about their work can enhance their intrinsic motivation and creativity. Freedom to explore new ideas and approaches encourages experimentation and innovation.

2. Resources: Adequate resources, including time, funding, and access to information, are essential for supporting creative efforts. Resource constraints can stifle creativity, while well-resourced environments can facilitate it.

3. Supportive Leadership: Leaders who encourage and recognize creativity, provide constructive feedback, and foster a culture of trust and psychological safety can significantly enhance individual and collective creativity.

4. Organizational Climate: A work environment characterized by open communication, collaboration, and a tolerance for failure can promote creativity. Conversely, a climate of fear and rigid control can inhibit creative expression.

Rosabeth Moss Kanter's Model of Innovation

Rosabeth Moss Kanter, a prominent scholar in organizational behavior, offers a model that focuses on the structural and cultural aspects of organizations that support innovation. Kanter's model identifies several key factors that contribute to an organization's ability to innovate:

- Diverse Teams: Kanter emphasizes the importance of diversity within teams. Diverse teams bring together different perspectives, experiences, and problem-solving approaches, which can lead to more creative and innovative solutions. Encouraging cross-functional collaboration and inclusivity can enhance the innovation potential of teams.

- Open Communication: Effective communication channels are crucial for sharing ideas and knowledge across the organization. Kanter highlights the need for open communication systems that facilitate the free flow of information and ideas. This openness helps break down silos and fosters a culture of collaboration and innovation.

- Culture of Experimentation: Kanter argues that organizations need to create a culture that values experimentation and learning from failure. Encouraging employees to take risks, experiment with new ideas, and learn from setbacks can drive continuous innovation. A culture that punishes failure, on the other hand, can stifle creativity and discourage employees from pursuing innovative initiatives.

- Leadership Support: Like Amabile, Kanter underscores the role of leadership in fostering innovation. Leaders need to champion innovation by providing vision, resources, and support for innovative projects. They should also create an environment where employees feel empowered to contribute their ideas and take initiative.

- Integrative Structures: Kanter points out that integrative structures, such as cross-functional teams, task forces, and innovation hubs, can facilitate collaboration and innovation. These structures help bring together diverse perspectives and expertise, enabling the organization to address complex challenges and seize new opportunities.

Practical Example: Google

Google is a prime example of an organization that embodies the principles of both Amabile's and Kanter's models. The company's famous "20% time" policy allows employees to spend 20% of their work time on projects they are passionate about, fostering intrinsic motivation and creativity. Google's open and collaborative culture, supported by diverse teams and integrative structures, encourages the free flow of ideas and experimentation. Leadership at Google actively supports innovation by providing resources and creating an environment where failure is seen as a learning opportunity.

Both Amabile and Kanter provide valuable frameworks for understanding and fostering innovation within organizations. Amabile's model emphasizes the importance of individual creativity and the organizational environment, while Kanter's model focuses on structural and cultural factors that support innovation. By integrating insights from both models, organizations can create environments that nurture creativity, encourage experimentation, and drive continuous innovation. As you consider these models, reflect on how their principles can be applied to enhance innovation within your own organization.

Conditions for Successful Innovation

Creating an environment where innovation thrives requires careful attention to a variety of conditions that support and encourage the creative process. Organizations that cultivate these conditions can foster a culture of continuous improvement and adaptation, driving long-term success and competitiveness. Here are the essential conditions for successful innovation:

1. Supportive Organizational Culture

A supportive culture is fundamental to fostering innovation. This culture values creativity, risk-taking, and learning from failure. Employees should feel safe to express their ideas without fear of ridicule or retribution. This psychological safety encourages experimentation and the pursuit of novel solutions.

Practical Example: At Pixar, the culture is built around the belief that creativity requires vulnerability and the freedom to fail. The company promotes an environment where employees are encouraged to share their rough ideas and receive constructive feedback, fostering a rich exchange of creative concepts.

2. Leadership Commitment

Leadership plays a crucial role in promoting and sustaining innovation. Leaders must be committed to innovation, demonstrating support through their actions and decisions. This includes providing resources, setting a clear vision for innovation, and actively participating in the innovation process.

Practical Example: Jeff Bezos of Amazon is known for his commitment to innovation. He promotes a long-term vision for the company, encourages experimentation, and is willing to invest in new and unproven ideas, understanding that not all will succeed but some will lead to significant breakthroughs.

3. Adequate Resources

Innovation requires resources, including time, funding, and access to information. Organizations must allocate sufficient resources to support innovative projects and ensure that employees have the tools and information they need to develop and implement new ideas.

Practical Example: Google's "20% time" policy, where employees are allowed to spend 20% of their work time on projects they are passionate about, provides the necessary time and freedom for employees to explore innovative ideas without the pressure of immediate returns.

4. Cross-Functional Collaboration

Innovation often arises from the intersection of diverse perspectives and expertise. Encouraging collaboration across different departments and functions can lead to the generation of novel ideas and more comprehensive solutions to complex problems.

Practical Example: 3M's innovation culture is heavily reliant on cross-functional collaboration. The company's practice of rotating employees across different roles and departments helps to cross-pollinate ideas and foster a collaborative approach to innovation.

5. Open Communication

Open and transparent communication channels are essential for fostering innovation. Employees should be encouraged to share their ideas and feedback, and there should be mechanisms in place to facilitate the flow of information and ideas throughout the organization.

Practical Example: At IDEO, an international design and consulting firm, open communication is a core value. The company uses a variety of tools and practices, such as brainstorming sessions and open office layouts, to encourage the free exchange of ideas among employees.

6. Risk-Taking and Tolerance for Failure

Innovation involves taking risks, and not all ideas will succeed. Organizations must foster an environment where risk-taking is encouraged and failure is viewed as a learning opportunity rather than a setback. This tolerance for failure can significantly enhance the innovation process.

Practical Example: Elon Musk's companies, including Tesla and SpaceX, exemplify a high tolerance for risk and failure. Both companies have faced significant setbacks, but their willingness to take bold risks has also led to groundbreaking innovations and advancements.

7. Continuous Learning and Development

An environment that promotes continuous learning and development helps employees to stay up-to-date with the latest trends, technologies, and best practices. Providing opportunities for professional growth and development can enhance employees' creative and innovative capabilities.

Practical Example: IBM invests heavily in continuous learning and development for its employees. The company offers extensive training programs and encourages employees to pursue further education, ensuring that the workforce is equipped with the latest knowledge and skills to drive innovation.

8. Clear Vision and Strategic Alignment

Having a clear vision for innovation that aligns with the organization's overall strategy is crucial. This ensures that innovative efforts are focused and directed towards achieving strategic objectives, rather than being scattered or misaligned with the organization's goals.

Practical Example: Apple's innovation strategy is closely aligned with its vision of creating products that enrich people's lives. This clear vision guides all innovation efforts within the company, ensuring that new products and services align with the brand's overarching mission and strategic goals.

9. Customer-Centric Approach

Innovation should be driven by a deep understanding of customer needs and preferences. Organizations that prioritize customer feedback and involve customers in the innovation process are more likely to develop solutions that meet market demands and create value.

Practical Example: Procter & Gamble (P&G) employs a customer-centric approach to innovation through its "Connect + Develop" program, which involves customers and external partners in the development of new products. This approach helps P&G to tailor its innovations to meet the specific needs and preferences of its customers.

10. Structured Innovation Processes

Implementing structured processes for managing innovation can help to systematically identify, develop, and implement new ideas. This includes having clear stages for idea generation, evaluation, development, and commercialization, as well as mechanisms for tracking progress and measuring outcomes.

Practical Example: Intel's structured innovation process, known as the "Intel Labs Innovation Pipeline," ensures that ideas are systematically evaluated and developed. The process includes stages such as ideation, prototyping, testing, and scaling, with defined criteria for moving ideas from one stage to the next.

Fostering a culture of innovation requires creating an environment that supports creativity, risk-taking, and continuous learning. By ensuring that the conditions outlined above are in place, organizations can cultivate a culture that not only encourages the generation of new ideas but also effectively develops and implements innovative solutions. As you consider these conditions, think about how they can be applied within your organization to enhance its capacity for innovation and drive long-term success.

Successful organizational innovation often hinges on the ability to create environments that nurture creativity, risk-taking, and collaboration. Several companies have exemplified these principles, achieving remarkable innovation through thoughtful strategies and practices.

Pixar, a leader in animated filmmaking, provides a compelling case study. From its inception, Pixar has fostered a culture that encourages creativity and open communication. The company's "Braintrust" meetings are a cornerstone of this approach. In these sessions, directors present their work-in-progress to a group of peers who provide candid feedback. The key to these meetings is the trust and respect among participants, allowing for honest critiques without fear of judgment. This practice helps refine ideas and ensures high-quality output. Pixar also emphasizes the importance of learning from failure. The company views mistakes as integral to the creative process, encouraging teams to take risks and explore bold ideas without fear of repercussions. This tolerance for failure has led to groundbreaking films that push the boundaries of animation and storytelling.

Another notable example is Google, which has institutionalized innovation through various initiatives. The "20% time" policy allows employees to dedicate 20% of their workweek to projects they are passionate about, irrespective of their direct job responsibilities. This freedom has led to the creation of highly successful products like Gmail and Google Maps. Google also promotes a culture of collaboration and openness. Its open office layouts and numerous communal spaces encourage spontaneous interactions and idea sharing. The company uses internal platforms like "Google Moderator" to crowdsource ideas and feedback from employees worldwide, ensuring diverse perspectives contribute to innovation. By providing ample resources, maintaining an open communication culture, and allowing freedom to explore, Google continuously generates innovative solutions and maintains its competitive edge.

3M's innovation journey is another insightful case. The company, known for its culture of innovation, encourages cross-functional collaboration and a bottom-up approach to idea generation. One of 3M's most famous innovations, the Post-it Note, originated from an employee's failed attempt to develop a strong adhesive. Instead of discarding the idea, 3M allowed the employee to explore its potential, leading to the creation of a product that revolutionized office supplies. 3M's "15% rule" is similar to Google's approach, permitting employees to spend a portion of their time on projects outside their regular responsibilities. This policy fosters a culture of experimentation and risk-taking. Moreover, 3M invests in internal innovation programs like "Genesis Grants," which provide funding for employees to pursue innovative ideas. These practices ensure that innovation is embedded in the company's DNA, leading to continuous development of new products and technologies.

Amazon's approach to innovation offers another illustrative example. Jeff Bezos has ingrained a culture of customer obsession and long-term thinking into Amazon's core values. The company's strategy involves working backwards from the customer's needs, ensuring that every innovation adds genuine value. This customer-centric approach led to the creation of services like Amazon Prime, AWS, and Kindle, which have transformed entire industries. Amazon also practices "two-pizza teams," small, autonomous groups that can be fed with two pizzas, to maintain agility and focus. These teams are empowered to make decisions quickly and innovate without bureaucratic constraints.

This structural approach allows Amazon to rapidly prototype, test, and scale new ideas, maintaining its position as a leader in e-commerce and technology.

Tesla, under the leadership of Elon Musk, demonstrates how a bold vision and risk-taking can drive innovation in a traditionally slow-moving industry like automotive manufacturing. Tesla's commitment to electric vehicles, energy storage, and renewable energy solutions is rooted in a mission to accelerate the world's transition to sustainable energy. The company's innovative approach includes vertically integrating manufacturing processes and continuously updating its vehicles through over-the-air software updates. Tesla's "gigafactories" are massive production facilities designed to scale the production of batteries and electric vehicles efficiently. By investing heavily in research and development, embracing risk, and maintaining a clear long-term vision, Tesla has disrupted the automotive industry and established itself as a leader in sustainable technology.

Each of these case studies highlights the importance of creating environments that support and encourage innovation. Whether through fostering a culture of open communication, providing resources and time for exploration, emphasizing collaboration, or maintaining a customer-centric approach, these organizations demonstrate that innovation is not just about having great ideas but also about creating the right conditions for those ideas to flourish. By adopting similar strategies, other organizations can enhance their capacity for innovation, driving growth and maintaining competitiveness in an ever-evolving market.

Innovation is the engine of growth and competitiveness in today's fast-paced and ever-changing business environment. Through the exploration of various models and real-world case studies, we have seen how critical it is for organizations to cultivate environments that nurture creativity, risk-taking, and collaboration.

Teresa Amabile's model emphasizes the need for intrinsic motivation, domain-relevant skills, and creativity-relevant processes. It shows how individual creativity, supported by a conducive organizational environment, can lead to innovative outcomes. Rosabeth Moss Kanter's model further underscores the importance of structural and cultural factors, such as diverse teams, open communication, and a tolerance for failure, in fostering a climate where innovation can thrive.

Successful innovation requires a delicate balance of several conditions. A supportive organizational culture that encourages experimentation and learning from failure is fundamental. Leadership commitment is crucial, as leaders set the tone and provide the necessary resources and vision. Adequate resources, including time, funding, and information, enable employees to explore and develop new ideas. Cross-functional collaboration brings diverse perspectives together, enhancing the creative process. Open communication ensures that ideas flow freely throughout the organization, breaking down silos and fostering a collaborative spirit. Risk-taking and a tolerance for failure are essential for encouraging employees to experiment without fear of negative consequences. Continuous learning and development ensure that employees are equipped with the latest knowledge and skills. A clear vision for innovation aligned with the organization's strategic goals provides direction and focus. A customer-centric approach ensures that innovations meet market needs and create value. Finally, structured innovation processes help systematically manage the journey from idea generation to implementation.

The case studies of Pixar, Google, 3M, Amazon, and Tesla illustrate how these conditions can be practically applied to achieve remarkable innovation. These organizations demonstrate that fostering a culture of innovation requires more than just encouraging creativity—it involves creating an ecosystem where innovative ideas can be nurtured, developed, and brought to market successfully.

As we conclude this chapter on innovation, it is clear that the ability to innovate is not confined to a few exceptional companies. Any organization can cultivate an innovative environment by understanding and implementing the conditions that support creativity and experimentation. By fostering a culture that values diversity of thought, encourages open communication, and provides the necessary resources and leadership support, organizations can drive continuous innovation and achieve sustained success.

Reflecting on these insights, consider how your organization can enhance its innovation capabilities. Identify areas where you can improve cultural and structural support for innovation, invest in developing the necessary skills and processes, and create an environment where creativity and risk-taking are encouraged and rewarded. By doing so, you will be well-positioned to navigate the challenges of the future, capitalize on new opportunities, and maintain a competitive edge in an increasingly dynamic marketplace.

Chapter 10: Managing Change and Development

In today's rapidly evolving business landscape, the ability to manage change and drive development is essential for organizational survival and success. Organizations must continuously adapt to shifting market conditions, technological advancements, regulatory changes, and evolving customer expectations. Effective change management and development practices enable organizations to navigate these challenges, seize new opportunities, and maintain a competitive edge.

This chapter explores the critical aspects of managing organizational change and development, providing insights into the theories, strategies, and challenges associated with these processes. We begin by examining various theories of organizational change, which offer frameworks for understanding how change occurs and how it can be managed effectively. These theories provide valuable insights into the dynamics of change, highlighting the importance of planning, communication, and stakeholder engagement.

We explore strategies for effective change management, focusing on practical approaches that leaders can employ to guide their organizations through transitions. These strategies emphasize the importance of clear communication, employee involvement, and continuous feedback. By adopting a structured and empathetic approach to change management, leaders can minimize resistance, foster buy-in, and ensure successful implementation of change initiatives. Additionally, we will address the unique challenges faced by organizations in different sectors, with a particular focus on healthcare. The healthcare industry, characterized by its complexity, regulatory constraints, and high stakes, presents unique challenges for change management. We will explore specific strategies and case studies that highlight how healthcare organizations have successfully navigated these challenges, offering lessons that can be applied across various sectors.

So as we investigate these intricacies of managing change and development, consider how these principles and strategies can be applied within your own organization. Reflect on past change initiatives, identify areas for improvement, and think about how you can better prepare for future changes. This chapter aims to equip you with the knowledge and tools needed to lead your organization through change effectively, fostering a culture of continuous development and resilience.

Theories of Organizational Change

Understanding the theories of organizational change is essential for effectively navigating and implementing change within any organization. These theories provide frameworks that help leaders and managers comprehend the dynamics of change and the factors that influence its success or failure. Several key theories offer valuable insights into the processes and principles of organizational change.

Kurt Lewin's Change Management Model is one of the most influential and foundational theories in the field of organizational change. Lewin conceptualized change as a process that involves three key stages: unfreezing, changing, and refreezing. In the unfreezing stage, the organization prepares for change by recognizing the need for it and creating a sense of urgency. This stage involves dismantling existing mindsets and overcoming resistance to change. The changing stage is where the actual transition occurs. New processes, behaviors, and ways of thinking are implemented. During this phase, effective communication and support are crucial to help employees adapt to the changes. The final stage, refreezing, involves solidifying the new changes into the organization's culture and practices, ensuring that the changes are sustained over time. This model emphasizes the importance of preparing the organization for change, managing the transition effectively, and reinforcing the new ways of working to achieve lasting benefits.

John Kotter's 8-Step Process for Leading Change provides a more detailed and structured approach to organizational change. Kotter's model outlines eight essential steps for successful change: creating a sense of urgency, forming a powerful coalition, developing a vision and strategy, communicating the change vision, empowering employees for broad-based action, generating short-term wins, consolidating gains to produce more change, and anchoring new approaches in the culture. This model highlights the importance of strong leadership, clear vision, and ongoing communication throughout the change process. By following these steps, organizations can build momentum, overcome resistance, and embed new practices into their culture.

The ADKAR Model, developed by Prosci, focuses on the individual aspects of change and how employees experience it. ADKAR stands for Awareness, Desire, Knowledge, Ability, and Reinforcement. According to this model, successful change occurs when individuals move through these stages. Awareness involves understanding why change is necessary. Desire represents the individual's willingness to support and participate in the change. Knowledge is the information and training needed to implement the change. Ability refers to the individual's capacity to apply new skills and behaviors. Reinforcement involves ensuring that the changes are maintained over time through ongoing support and recognition. The ADKAR Model emphasizes the need to address individual concerns and motivations to achieve successful organizational change.

The McKinsey 7-S Framework is another valuable tool for understanding organizational change. This model identifies seven interconnected elements that need to be aligned for successful change: strategy, structure, systems, shared values, skills, style, and staff. According to the 7-S Framework, effective change requires attention to all these elements and how they interact. For example, changes in strategy may necessitate adjustments in organizational structure, systems, and skills. By considering the alignment of these elements, organizations can ensure a holistic approach to change that addresses multiple dimensions of the organization.

Another important theory is the Lewin's Force Field Analysis, which provides a method for analyzing the forces that support or hinder change. According to this theory, change is a result of the balance between driving forces (factors that push for change) and restraining forces (factors that resist change). Successful change occurs when driving forces outweigh restraining forces. By identifying and analyzing these forces, leaders can develop strategies to strengthen driving forces and reduce or eliminate restraining forces. This analysis helps to create a more supportive environment for change and addresses potential barriers proactively.

William Bridges' Transition Model focuses on the psychological aspects of change, emphasizing the human side of organizational transitions. Bridges distinguishes between change, which is situational, and transition, which is psychological. His model outlines three stages of transition: ending, losing, and letting go; the neutral zone; and the new beginning. The first stage involves helping individuals let go of the old ways and deal with the losses associated with change. The neutral zone is a period of uncertainty and exploration, where individuals are between the old and the new. The final stage, the new beginning, involves embracing the new ways and developing a new identity and sense of purpose. This model highlights the emotional and psychological journey that individuals experience during change and underscores the importance of supporting employees through these transitions.

These theories of organizational change provide valuable insights into the processes, principles, and human aspects of change. Understanding these models helps leaders and managers navigate the complexities of change, address resistance, and implement strategies that foster successful transitions. By applying these theories, organizations can enhance their capacity for change, achieve their strategic goals, and create a culture of continuous improvement and adaptability.

Strategies for Effective Change Management

Successfully managing change within an organization requires a thoughtful and structured approach. Effective change management strategies ensure that transitions are smooth, stakeholders are engaged, and the desired outcomes are achieved. Here are several key strategies that can help leaders and managers navigate change effectively:

First, develop a clear vision and strategy for change. Articulate the reasons for the change, the expected benefits, and how it aligns with the organization's long-term goals. A clear vision provides direction and motivation, helping employees understand the purpose and importance of the change. Communicate this vision consistently and persuasively to create a shared sense of urgency and commitment.

Engage and involve stakeholders early in the process. Successful change management requires the support and participation of those affected by the change. Identify key stakeholders, including employees, customers, and partners, and involve them in planning and decision-making. This involvement fosters ownership and reduces resistance, as stakeholders feel their concerns and ideas are valued.

Effective communication is crucial throughout the change process. Develop a comprehensive communication plan that includes regular updates, feedback channels, and opportunities for dialogue. Transparency is key—ensure that information about the change is clear, consistent, and accessible. Address concerns and questions promptly to build trust and reduce uncertainty.

Provide training and support to help employees adapt to the change. Change often requires new skills, behaviors, and ways of working. Assess the training needs and develop programs that equip employees with the necessary knowledge and competencies. Additionally, offer support through coaching, mentoring, and resources that help employees navigate the transition.

Empower employees to take action and make decisions that support the change. Encourage initiative and innovation by giving employees the authority and resources to implement changes within their areas of responsibility. Empowerment increases engagement and fosters a culture of accountability and ownership.

Generate and celebrate short-term wins. Achieving quick, visible successes early in the change process can build momentum and reinforce commitment. Identify and implement achievable milestones that demonstrate progress. Recognize and reward the efforts of individuals and teams who contribute to these successes, highlighting how their actions align with the overall vision.

Monitor progress and adjust as needed. Change processes rarely go exactly as planned. Establish metrics and feedback mechanisms to track progress and identify areas where adjustments are necessary. Be flexible and responsive, making course corrections to address challenges and capitalize on new opportunities.

Foster a culture of continuous improvement. Change should not be viewed as a one-time event but as an ongoing process. Encourage a mindset of learning and adaptation, where employees continuously seek ways to improve and innovate. This culture of continuous improvement enhances the organization's resilience and ability to respond to future changes.

Provide strong and visible leadership throughout the change process. Leaders play a critical role in guiding the organization through change. They must demonstrate commitment, model desired behaviors, and provide support and direction. Visible and accessible leaders who communicate openly and act decisively can inspire confidence and trust.

Address the human side of change by recognizing and managing the emotional and psychological impact on employees. Change can be stressful and unsettling. Provide opportunities for employees to express their feelings and concerns. Offer support through counseling, employee assistance programs, and stress management resources. Acknowledge the personal and professional challenges employees may face and show empathy and understanding.

Consider a practical example from the healthcare sector. A hospital undergoing a major transition to implement a new electronic health records (EHR) system can apply these strategies effectively. The hospital leadership begins by clearly communicating the vision for the new EHR system, emphasizing improved patient care and operational efficiency. Stakeholders, including doctors, nurses, administrative staff, and patients, are involved in the planning process, ensuring their input shapes the implementation strategy.

Comprehensive training programs are developed to equip staff with the necessary skills to use the new system effectively. Regular updates and open forums are provided to address concerns and questions. Short-term wins, such as successful pilot tests in specific departments, are celebrated and communicated throughout the hospital to build momentum.

Leaders remain visible and actively engaged, demonstrating their commitment to the change. Progress is monitored through key performance indicators, and adjustments are made based on feedback and performance data. By addressing both the technical and emotional aspects of the change, the hospital successfully transitions to the new EHR system, achieving its goals of enhanced patient care and streamlined operations.

Effective change management requires a holistic and strategic approach. By developing a clear vision, engaging stakeholders, communicating effectively, providing training and support, empowering employees, celebrating short-term wins, monitoring progress, fostering continuous improvement, and addressing the human side of change, organizations can navigate transitions successfully and achieve their desired outcomes. These strategies help create a resilient organization that is capable of adapting to change and thriving in a dynamic environment.

Challenges in Healthcare and Other Sectors

Managing change in any sector can be complex, but healthcare presents unique challenges due to its inherent complexity, regulatory environment, and high stakes. Other sectors also face distinct obstacles that must be navigated for successful change management. Understanding these challenges is crucial for developing effective strategies tailored to each sector's specific needs.

Healthcare Sector

The healthcare sector faces significant challenges in managing change due to the complexity of its operations, the critical nature of its services, and the stringent regulatory environment. One major challenge is the integration of new technologies, such as electronic health records (EHR), telemedicine, and advanced diagnostic tools. Implementing these technologies requires substantial investments in infrastructure and training, as well as changes in workflows and processes. Resistance from staff, who may be accustomed to traditional methods, can hinder the adoption of new technologies.

Another challenge in healthcare is ensuring patient safety and maintaining high standards of care during transitions. Any change in procedures or systems can introduce risks, making it essential to implement rigorous training and oversight to prevent errors. Additionally, the sector is highly regulated, with stringent compliance requirements that can complicate change initiatives. Healthcare organizations must navigate complex regulatory frameworks to ensure that any changes comply with laws and standards, which can slow down the implementation process.

The emotional and psychological impact of change on healthcare professionals is another critical factor. Healthcare workers often operate under high stress and intense pressure. Introducing changes can add to this stress, leading to burnout and resistance. Effective change management in healthcare must include robust support systems to help staff adapt and cope with new demands.

Technology Sector

In the technology sector, rapid innovation and market competition create a fast-paced environment where continuous change is necessary. One challenge is managing the pace of innovation while maintaining operational stability. Technology companies must balance the need to develop and release new products quickly with the requirement to ensure quality and reliability.

Another challenge is talent management. The tech industry is characterized by high employee mobility, with skilled professionals frequently moving between companies. Retaining talent during periods of change requires strong leadership, clear communication, and creating a culture that values and supports employees.

Cybersecurity is a critical concern in the technology sector. Implementing new technologies and processes can introduce vulnerabilities that need to be managed proactively. Ensuring that change initiatives do not compromise security is essential for maintaining customer trust and protecting sensitive data.

Financial Services Sector

The financial services sector faces unique challenges related to regulatory compliance, risk management, and technological advancements. Regulatory changes often necessitate significant adjustments to processes, systems, and practices. Financial institutions must stay abreast of evolving regulations and ensure that their change initiatives comply with all legal requirements.

Risk management is another critical challenge. Financial institutions must carefully assess and mitigate risks associated with changes, particularly those involving new financial products, services, or technologies. Failure to manage risks effectively can lead to financial losses, reputational damage, and legal repercussions.

Digital transformation is reshaping the financial services sector, requiring institutions to adopt new technologies such as blockchain, artificial intelligence, and mobile banking solutions.

Implementing these technologies involves overcoming resistance from employees and customers who may be wary of new systems. Ensuring a smooth transition requires comprehensive training, clear communication, and robust technical support.

Manufacturing Sector

In the manufacturing sector, change management challenges often revolve around process optimization, technology adoption, and workforce adaptation. Implementing new manufacturing technologies, such as automation, robotics, and advanced analytics, requires significant capital investment and changes to production processes. These changes can disrupt existing workflows and necessitate retraining of employees.

Supply chain management is another area where change can be challenging. Manufacturers must coordinate changes across a complex network of suppliers, distributors, and partners. Ensuring alignment and minimizing disruptions in the supply chain is critical for maintaining production schedules and meeting customer demands.

Workforce adaptation is a significant challenge, particularly with the increasing automation of manufacturing processes. Employees may fear job loss or struggle to adapt to new roles that require different skills. Effective change management must include strategies for reskilling and upskilling the workforce, providing support and reassurance to employees.

Retail Sector

The retail sector faces challenges related to changing consumer behaviors, technological advancements, and supply chain logistics. The rise of e-commerce and omnichannel retailing requires traditional retailers to adapt their business models and invest in new technologies. Integrating online and offline operations, managing inventory in real-time, and ensuring a seamless customer experience across channels are complex tasks.

Consumer behavior is constantly evolving, driven by trends such as personalized shopping experiences, sustainability, and convenience. Retailers must stay attuned to these changes and adapt their strategies accordingly. This requires agility and a willingness to experiment with new approaches to meet customer expectations.

Supply chain logistics in the retail sector are increasingly complex, with the need to manage global networks, ensure timely delivery, and handle returns efficiently. Changes in supply chain processes can have widespread impacts, requiring careful planning and coordination to avoid disruptions.

Each sector presents unique challenges for managing change, but common themes include the need for strong leadership, clear communication, employee involvement, and comprehensive training and support. Understanding the specific obstacles faced by different industries allows organizations to tailor their change management strategies effectively. By addressing these challenges proactively, organizations can navigate transitions successfully, minimize disruptions, and achieve their strategic objectives.

Part VI: Contemporary Issues and Future Directions

In an era of unprecedented change and complexity, organizations face a host of contemporary challenges and opportunities that shape their strategies, structures, and practices. As we move forward, understanding these contemporary issues and anticipating future directions is crucial for organizational success. Part VI of this book revolves around the impact of globalization, emerging trends in organizational theory, and the critical role of technology, sustainability, and ethics in shaping the future of organizations.

Chapter 11 explores the profound impact of globalization on organizational theory and practice. Globalization has reshaped the way organizations operate, breaking down geographical boundaries and creating a more interconnected world. This chapter examines how globalization influences organizational structures, necessitating adaptations to diverse markets and cultures. We will discuss the challenges and strategies for organizations to thrive in a globalized environment, emphasizing the importance of cultural sensitivity, global integration, and local responsiveness.

Chapter 12 looks ahead to future trends in organizational theory, focusing on emerging concepts and technologies that are transforming the business landscape. We will explore how technology, including blockchain and artificial intelligence, is revolutionizing organizational processes, decision-making, and competitive dynamics. These technologies offer new opportunities for efficiency, transparency, and innovation but also present significant challenges and ethical considerations.

Sustainable and ethical organizational practices are increasingly becoming central to organizational theory and practice. As stakeholders demand greater accountability and social responsibility, organizations must integrate sustainability and ethics into their core strategies. This chapter will highlight the importance of adopting sustainable practices and ethical frameworks to ensure long-term success and positive societal impact.

As we navigate these contemporary issues and future directions, consider how your organization can adapt and thrive in a rapidly changing world. Reflect on the implications of globalization, emerging technologies, and the growing emphasis on sustainability and ethics. By understanding and addressing these critical areas, you can position your organization for sustained success in an increasingly complex and dynamic environment.

Chapter 11: Globalization and Organizational Theory

Globalization has fundamentally transformed the way organizations operate, compelling them to rethink and often redesign their structures to compete effectively in an interconnected world. The removal of geographical barriers, advances in technology, and the integration of global markets have led to significant changes in organizational structures, which are now more complex, flexible, and dynamic than ever before.

One of the most notable impacts of globalization on organizational structures is the shift towards more decentralized and geographically dispersed models. Traditional hierarchical structures, with centralized decision-making, have given way to more flexible and adaptive configurations. Multinational corporations, for instance, often adopt a matrix structure, where employees report to multiple managers across different dimensions such as product lines, geographical regions, and functional areas. This allows organizations to respond more effectively to local market conditions while maintaining global coordination and integration.

The matrix structure facilitates the sharing of resources and expertise across different parts of the organization, promoting innovation and efficiency. However, it also introduces complexities in communication and decision-making, requiring robust coordination mechanisms and clear roles and responsibilities to avoid confusion and conflicts.

Another significant change driven by globalization is the rise of networked and virtual organizational structures. Advances in communication technologies enable organizations to build global networks of partners, suppliers, and customers. These networked structures allow organizations to leverage external capabilities and resources, fostering collaboration and innovation across borders. Virtual teams, consisting of members from different locations and time zones, are increasingly common, enabling organizations to operate around the clock and tap into a diverse talent pool.

These networked and virtual structures offer several advantages, including flexibility, agility, and access to a broader range of skills and perspectives. However, they also pose challenges related to coordination, trust, and cultural differences. Effective management of virtual teams requires strong communication practices, cultural sensitivity, and the use of technology to bridge gaps and facilitate collaboration.

Globalization also drives organizations to adopt more modular and scalable structures. In a rapidly changing global market, the ability to quickly reconfigure organizational units and processes is crucial. Modular structures, where units operate semi-autonomously but are connected through standardized interfaces, allow organizations to adapt more swiftly to changes in the external environment. This approach supports innovation and responsiveness by enabling different parts of the organization to experiment and develop new capabilities independently while ensuring coherence and integration at the corporate level.

The need to manage diverse workforces across different cultural and regulatory environments has also led to changes in organizational structures. Global organizations must navigate varying legal requirements, labor practices, and cultural norms. This complexity requires structures that balance global consistency with local adaptation. Many organizations adopt a transnational structure, which combines global coordination with local responsiveness. In this model, decision-making is distributed across global and local units, allowing the organization to leverage global efficiencies while remaining sensitive to local market needs.

A practical example of the impact of globalization on organizational structures is seen in companies like Unilever and Procter & Gamble. These consumer goods giants have restructured their organizations to operate efficiently in diverse markets worldwide. They have implemented matrix structures to balance product line management with regional market demands, enabling them to tailor their products and marketing strategies to local preferences while maintaining global brand coherence and operational efficiency.

Another example is IBM, which has transitioned from a traditional hierarchical structure to a globally integrated enterprise. IBM's structure now includes global centers of excellence and integrated delivery centers that serve clients worldwide. This transformation allows IBM to optimize its resources globally, enhance innovation through collaboration, and provide consistent service quality across different regions.

Globalization has significantly impacted organizational structures, driving the shift towards more decentralized, networked, modular, and transnational models. These changes enable organizations to operate more flexibly and responsively in a complex and dynamic global environment. However, they also introduce challenges related to coordination, communication, and cultural integration. By understanding and addressing these challenges, organizations can effectively harness the opportunities presented by globalization, ensuring sustained competitiveness and growth in the global marketplace. As organizations continue to evolve, the ability to adapt their structures to the demands of globalization will remain a critical factor for success.

Adapting to Global Markets and Cultures

Adapting to global markets and cultures is a critical success factor for organizations operating in today's interconnected world. The diversity of cultural norms, consumer preferences, regulatory environments, and economic conditions across different countries requires organizations to be flexible and culturally sensitive. Successfully navigating these differences can enhance competitive advantage, foster customer loyalty, and drive global growth. Here's how organizations can effectively adapt to global markets and cultures:

Understanding Cultural Differences

One of the first steps in adapting to global markets is gaining a deep understanding of cultural differences. Culture shapes consumer behavior, communication styles, and business practices. Organizations must invest in cultural intelligence to effectively engage with diverse markets. This involves learning about local customs, values, and traditions, as well as understanding how these factors influence purchasing decisions and brand perceptions. For example, Hofstede's Cultural Dimensions Theory can be a useful tool for analyzing cultural differences. This framework examines cultural variations across dimensions such as power distance, individualism vs. collectivism, masculinity vs. femininity, uncertainty avoidance, long-term vs. short-term orientation, and indulgence vs. restraint. By understanding where a particular culture falls on these dimensions, organizations can tailor their strategies to align with local expectations and norms.

Customizing Products and Services

To resonate with local consumers, organizations often need to customize their products and services. This might involve adapting product features, packaging, branding, and marketing messages to suit local tastes and preferences. Customization shows respect for local cultures and increases the relevance of the offerings, thereby enhancing market acceptance and customer satisfaction.

A notable example is McDonald's, which adapts its menu to cater to local tastes in different countries. In India, McDonald's offers a range of vegetarian options and dishes like the McAloo Tikki burger to appeal to local dietary preferences. Similarly, in Japan, the menu includes items like the Teriyaki Burger and Ebi Filet-O (shrimp burger) that cater to local tastes. These adaptations have helped McDonald's build a strong global presence while respecting and celebrating cultural diversity.

Localizing Marketing and Communication

Effective communication is essential for connecting with global audiences. This requires localizing marketing strategies and messages to resonate with different cultural contexts. Localization goes beyond translation; it involves adapting content to reflect cultural nuances, values, and idioms. This can make marketing efforts more relatable and impactful, fostering stronger connections with local consumers.

Coca-Cola's "Share a Coke" campaign, which involved printing popular names on Coke bottles, was adapted differently in various countries to reflect local naming conventions and cultural preferences. In China, where individualism is less emphasized, Coca-Cola printed popular phrases that promoted social harmony and collective joy. This localized approach helped Coca-Cola connect with diverse audiences on a personal and cultural level.

Building Local Partnerships

Collaborating with local partners can provide valuable insights and facilitate smoother market entry. Local partners bring knowledge of the local market, regulatory environment, and cultural context, which can help organizations navigate complexities and avoid potential pitfalls. Partnerships can take various forms, including joint ventures, alliances, and collaborations with local suppliers, distributors, and marketing agencies.

Starbucks' entry into the Chinese market was facilitated by partnerships with local companies. These collaborations helped Starbucks understand local consumer preferences and adapt its offerings accordingly. By working with local partners, Starbucks was able to design store environments and menu items that resonated with Chinese consumers, such as offering tea-based beverages and incorporating local architectural elements into store designs.

Adapting Organizational Structures

Global expansion often necessitates changes in organizational structures to balance global integration with local responsiveness. Companies may adopt matrix structures, regional divisions, or transnational models that allow for both global coordination and local adaptation. These structures enable organizations to leverage global efficiencies while being agile enough to meet local market needs. A practical example is Unilever, which has adopted a hybrid organizational structure that combines global categories with local market operations. This allows Unilever to maintain consistency in its global brands while tailoring its products and marketing strategies to local preferences. By empowering local teams to make decisions that align with local market conditions, Unilever ensures that it remains relevant and competitive in diverse markets.

Navigating Regulatory Environments

Different countries have varying regulatory requirements that can impact product approvals, marketing practices, employment laws, and business operations. Organizations must be diligent in understanding and complying with these regulations to avoid legal issues and build trust with local stakeholders. This often involves working closely with legal experts and regulatory bodies to ensure compliance and adapt strategies as needed.

Pharmaceutical companies entering new markets must navigate complex regulatory approval processes for their products. This requires thorough understanding of local regulations, submission of detailed documentation, and often conducting additional clinical trials to meet local standards. By investing in regulatory compliance, companies can ensure that their products are safely and legally available in new markets.

Investing in Local Talent

Hiring and developing local talent is crucial for understanding and responding to local market dynamics. Local employees bring valuable insights into cultural norms, consumer behavior, and business practices. They can also help bridge cultural gaps between the global headquarters and local operations, facilitating smoother implementation of strategies and initiatives. Toyota's approach to local talent development is a prime example. In its global operations, Toyota emphasizes hiring and training local employees, ensuring that they understand the company's values and operational standards while also contributing local knowledge. This strategy has helped Toyota build strong, culturally aware teams that drive success in diverse markets.

Adapting to global markets and cultures requires a multifaceted approach that encompasses understanding cultural differences, customizing products and services, localizing marketing efforts, building local partnerships, adapting organizational structures, navigating regulatory environments, and investing in local talent. By embracing these strategies, organizations can effectively navigate the complexities of global markets, build strong connections with local consumers, and achieve sustained success on the international stage. As globalization continues to shape the business landscape, the ability to adapt and respond to diverse cultural and market dynamics will remain a key determinant of organizational success.

Future Trends in Globalization, AI and Blockchain, and Internet of Things (IoT) and Beyond

As we look towards the future, several key trends are poised to shape the landscape of globalization, technology, and organizational practices. Understanding these trends is essential for organizations to remain competitive, innovative, and responsive to changing market dynamics and technological advancements.

Globalization: Evolving Dynamics

Globalization continues to evolve, driven by advancements in technology, shifting economic power, and changing geopolitical landscapes. One significant trend is the rise of emerging markets, particularly in Asia, Africa, and Latin America. These regions are becoming increasingly important as sources of growth, innovation, and talent. Organizations must adapt by developing strategies that cater to the unique needs and opportunities in these markets, emphasizing local partnerships and culturally attuned business practices.

The concept of "glocalization" is gaining traction, where organizations integrate global strategies with local adaptations. This approach allows companies to leverage global efficiencies while remaining responsive to local preferences and conditions. As global supply chains become more complex, companies are also focusing on building resilience and sustainability into their operations. This involves diversifying supply sources, investing in local production capabilities, and adopting sustainable practices to mitigate risks and ensure long-term viability.

Artificial Intelligence (AI) and Machine Learning

AI and machine learning are revolutionizing industries by enabling automation, enhancing decision-making, and driving innovation. The future will see AI becoming more integrated into everyday business processes, with applications ranging from customer service chatbots to predictive analytics and autonomous systems. Organizations will leverage AI to gain deeper insights from data, optimize operations, and create personalized customer experiences.

One emerging trend is the development of explainable AI, which aims to make AI decision-making more transparent and understandable to users. This is crucial for building trust and ensuring ethical use of AI technologies. Additionally, AI ethics and governance will become increasingly important as organizations seek to address concerns related to bias, privacy, and accountability.

AI-driven automation will transform the workforce, leading to the creation of new job roles and the displacement of others. Organizations must invest in reskilling and upskilling their employees to prepare for this shift. Collaboration between humans and AI, known as augmented intelligence, will enhance human capabilities and drive innovation.

Blockchain Technology

Blockchain technology is poised to transform industries by providing secure, transparent, and decentralized solutions for various applications. In the financial sector, blockchain is already disrupting traditional banking and payment systems through cryptocurrencies and decentralized finance (DeFi) platforms. The future will see broader adoption of blockchain in areas such as supply chain management, healthcare, and digital identity verification.

One key trend is the rise of smart contracts, which are self-executing contracts with the terms of the agreement directly written into code. Smart contracts enable automated, trustless transactions and can streamline complex processes such as insurance claims, legal agreements, and real estate transactions.

Blockchain's potential for enhancing transparency and traceability in supply chains is another important trend. By providing an immutable record of transactions, blockchain can help organizations verify the authenticity of products, track their journey from origin to consumer, and ensure compliance with regulations. This is particularly valuable in industries such as food and pharmaceuticals, where traceability is critical for safety and quality assurance.

Internet of Things (IoT) and Beyond

The Internet of Things (IoT) is transforming how we interact with the physical world by connecting devices, sensors, and systems to the internet. This connectivity enables real-time data collection, monitoring, and control, leading to increased efficiency and new business models. The future will see the proliferation of IoT devices across various domains, from smart homes and cities to industrial automation and healthcare.

One significant trend is the development of edge computing, which involves processing data closer to the source rather than relying on centralized cloud servers. Edge computing reduces latency, enhances security, and enables real-time decision-making, making it ideal for applications such as autonomous vehicles, industrial automation, and remote healthcare.

IoT is also driving the evolution of smart cities, where interconnected systems enhance urban living through improved traffic management, energy efficiency, and public safety. These cities leverage IoT data to optimize resource allocation, reduce environmental impact, and enhance the quality of life for residents.

Beyond IoT, the convergence of technologies such as 5G, AI, and blockchain will further accelerate innovation. 5G networks will provide the high-speed connectivity required for advanced IoT applications, enabling seamless communication between devices. The integration of AI will enhance the capabilities of IoT systems by enabling predictive analytics, anomaly detection, and autonomous decision-making. Blockchain will add a layer of security and transparency, ensuring the integrity and trustworthiness of IoT data.

Sustainability and Ethical Practices

As the global community becomes more aware of environmental and social issues, sustainability and ethical practices will become central to organizational strategies. Companies are increasingly adopting sustainable business models that prioritize resource efficiency, renewable energy, and circular economy principles. This shift is driven by regulatory requirements, consumer demand, and the need to mitigate risks associated with climate change.

Organizations will also focus on corporate social responsibility (CSR) initiatives that address social and environmental challenges. These initiatives can enhance brand reputation, attract talent, and build trust with stakeholders. Ethical considerations, such as data privacy, human rights, and fair labor practices, will be integral to business operations and decision-making.

The future of globalization, technology, and organizational practices will be shaped by the dynamic interplay of these trends. Organizations that embrace and adapt to these changes will be better positioned to thrive in an increasingly complex and interconnected world. By leveraging advancements in AI, blockchain, and IoT, and prioritizing sustainability and ethical practices, companies can drive innovation, enhance operational efficiency, and create lasting value for their stakeholders. As we move forward, staying informed about these trends and being proactive in addressing their implications will be key to achieving sustained success and positive societal impact.

In this chapter, we explored the transformative trends of globalization, artificial intelligence (AI), blockchain technology, and the Internet of Things (IoT), examining their profound impacts on organizational structures and strategies. These advancements are reshaping how businesses operate, compete, and interact with their environments, necessitating a proactive and adaptive approach to change management and development.

Globalization continues to evolve, with emerging markets playing an increasingly significant role in the global economy. Organizations must adopt flexible structures that balance global integration with local responsiveness, leveraging the concept of "glocalization" to tailor their strategies to diverse market needs. Building resilience in global supply chains and fostering sustainability are also crucial as companies navigate the complexities of international operations.

AI and machine learning are revolutionizing industries by enhancing decision-making, automating processes, and driving innovation. The integration of explainable AI and ethical considerations is essential to building trust and ensuring responsible use of these technologies. Organizations must invest in reskilling their workforce to adapt to AI-driven changes and harness the potential of augmented intelligence.

Blockchain technology offers secure, transparent, and decentralized solutions, disrupting traditional industries and enabling new business models. Smart contracts and enhanced supply chain transparency are just a few examples of how blockchain can streamline operations and build trust. The adoption of blockchain will continue to expand, providing opportunities for innovation and efficiency across various sectors.

The IoT is transforming how we interact with the physical world, connecting devices and systems to enable real-time data collection and control. The development of edge computing, smart cities, and advanced industrial automation are key trends driving the evolution of IoT. The convergence of IoT with 5G, AI, and blockchain will further accelerate innovation, enhancing the capabilities and applications of connected systems.

Sustainability and ethical practices are becoming central to organizational strategies, driven by regulatory requirements, consumer demand, and the imperative to address environmental and social challenges. Companies that prioritize resource efficiency, renewable energy, and corporate social responsibility (CSR) initiatives will enhance their brand reputation, attract talent, and build trust with stakeholders.

As we move forward, it is clear that the future of organizations will be shaped by their ability to adapt to these dynamic trends. By understanding and leveraging the opportunities presented by globalization, AI, blockchain, and IoT, and by prioritizing sustainability and ethics, organizations can drive innovation, enhance operational efficiency, and create lasting value. Staying informed about these trends and being proactive in addressing their implications will be key to achieving sustained success and positive societal impact.

The landscape of organizational theory and practice is rapidly evolving. The ability to navigate and harness the potential of emerging trends and technologies will define the success of organizations in the future. As we conclude this chapter, reflect on how these trends impact your organization and consider the strategies needed to adapt, innovate, and thrive in an increasingly complex and interconnected world. By embracing change and fostering a culture of continuous improvement, organizations can position themselves for long-term success and contribute to a more sustainable and equitable global economy.

Chapter 12: Future Trends in Organizational Theory

The landscape of organizational theory continues to evolve, driven by emerging theories, technological advancements, and a growing emphasis on sustainability and ethics. Understanding these future trends is crucial for organizations aiming to remain competitive and responsive in an increasingly complex and dynamic environment. This chapter explores the cutting-edge developments that are shaping the future of organizational theory and practice.

We begin by examining emerging theories and concepts that provide fresh perspectives on how organizations operate and succeed. These new approaches challenge traditional models and offer innovative frameworks for understanding organizational behavior, leadership, and strategy. By exploring these theories, we gain insights into how organizations can better adapt to the fast-paced and ever-changing business landscape.

The role of technology, particularly blockchain and artificial intelligence (AI), is transforming organizations in profound ways. Blockchain technology offers decentralized, secure, and transparent solutions that can revolutionize various aspects of business operations, from supply chain management to financial transactions. AI, on the other hand, is driving automation, enhancing decision-making, and fostering innovation across industries. This chapter delves into how these technologies are being integrated into organizational practices and the implications they have for the future of work and business.

Sustainable and ethical organizational practices are becoming increasingly important as stakeholders demand greater accountability and responsibility from businesses. Organizations are recognizing the need to adopt sustainable practices that minimize environmental impact and promote social equity. Ethical considerations, such as data privacy, fair labor practices, and corporate governance, are also gaining prominence. We will explore how organizations can integrate sustainability and ethics into their core strategies to ensure long-term success and positive societal impact.

As we navigate these future trends, consider how your organization can leverage emerging theories, embrace technological advancements, and commit to sustainable and ethical practices. This chapter aims to provide you with the knowledge and tools needed to anticipate and respond to the evolving demands of the business world, positioning your organization for continued growth and relevance in the years to come.

Emerging Theories and Concepts

The field of organizational theory is constantly evolving, shaped by new insights and changing dynamics in the business environment. Emerging theories and concepts offer innovative frameworks for understanding and improving organizational effectiveness. These new approaches challenge traditional models, emphasizing adaptability, complexity, and the human aspects of organizational life. Here, we explore several emerging theories and concepts that are gaining traction and reshaping how organizations are understood and managed.

Complexity Theory

Complexity theory views organizations as complex adaptive systems characterized by dynamic interactions and non-linear relationships. Unlike traditional mechanistic models that see organizations as predictable and controllable, complexity theory recognizes the inherent unpredictability and interconnectedness of organizational elements. This perspective highlights the importance of adaptability, resilience, and emergent behavior in organizations.

Organizations are seen as ecosystems where small changes can lead to significant outcomes, a concept known as the butterfly effect. Leaders must focus on creating conditions that foster innovation and adaptability rather than attempting to control every aspect of the organization. This involves encouraging experimentation, learning from failures, and leveraging diverse perspectives to navigate uncertainty.

Theory U

Developed by Otto Scharmer, Theory U proposes a framework for leading profound change and innovation. The "U" process involves three main stages: sensing, presencing, and realizing. In the sensing stage, leaders immerse themselves in the current reality, listening deeply to stakeholders and understanding the broader system. The presencing stage involves retreating and reflecting, allowing new insights and ideas to emerge. Finally, in the realizing stage, leaders co-create innovative solutions and prototypes that address the challenges identified in the sensing stage.

Theory U emphasizes the importance of mindfulness, empathy, and collaboration in leadership. It encourages leaders to connect with their deeper intentions and aspirations, fostering a more holistic and transformative approach to organizational change.

Positive Organizational Scholarship (POS)

Positive Organizational Scholarship focuses on the strengths and virtues that enable individuals and organizations to thrive. It studies the factors that contribute to excellence, resilience, and well-being in the workplace. POS shifts the focus from addressing problems and deficits to amplifying positive deviance and high-performance practices.

Key concepts in POS include positive leadership, which involves fostering a supportive and empowering environment, and psychological capital, which comprises hope, efficacy, resilience, and optimism. By promoting positive practices and strengths-based development, organizations can enhance employee engagement, creativity, and overall performance.

Holacracy

Holacracy is a decentralized organizational model that distributes authority and decision-making across self-organizing teams rather than a traditional hierarchical structure. Developed by Brian Robertson, holacracy aims to increase agility, transparency, and employee empowerment.

In a holacratic organization, roles and responsibilities are clearly defined, and teams operate with a high degree of autonomy. Decision-making is based on structured processes, such as governance meetings, where teams regularly review and adjust their roles and policies. This approach allows organizations to adapt quickly to changes and leverage the collective intelligence of their members.

The Learning Organization

The concept of the learning organization, popularized by Peter Senge, emphasizes the importance of continuous learning and adaptability in achieving long-term success. Learning organizations are characterized by a culture that encourages curiosity, experimentation, and knowledge sharing. They invest in developing their employees' skills and capabilities, fostering an environment where learning is embedded in daily practices.

Key principles of the learning organization include systems thinking, which involves understanding the interconnectedness of organizational elements; personal mastery, where individuals strive for continuous self-improvement; and shared vision, which aligns the organization's goals with the aspirations of its members.

Design Thinking

Design thinking is an innovation methodology that focuses on understanding and solving complex problems from a human-centered perspective. It involves five key stages: empathize, define, ideate, prototype, and test. By deeply understanding the needs and experiences of users, design thinking encourages the creation of innovative and practical solutions.

Organizations adopting design thinking foster a culture of creativity and collaboration, where multidisciplinary teams work together to generate and refine ideas. This approach not only drives innovation but also enhances customer satisfaction by ensuring that solutions are closely aligned with user needs.

Agile Management

Originally developed for software development, agile management has become a popular approach for managing projects and processes in various industries. Agile emphasizes iterative development, flexibility, and customer collaboration. Teams work in short cycles, or sprints, to deliver small, incremental improvements that can be quickly tested and adjusted based on feedback.

Agile management encourages a culture of continuous improvement, where teams regularly reflect on their processes and outcomes to identify opportunities for enhancement. This approach enables organizations to respond swiftly to changing market conditions and customer demands, fostering a more adaptive and resilient organization.

Psychological Safety

Psychological safety, a concept introduced by Amy Edmondson, refers to an environment where employees feel safe to take risks, express their ideas, and make mistakes without fear of retribution. High levels of psychological safety are associated with greater innovation, learning, and team performance.

Creating a psychologically safe environment involves fostering trust, open communication, and respect among team members. Leaders play a crucial role in modeling inclusive behavior, encouraging diverse viewpoints, and responding constructively to feedback. By promoting psychological safety, organizations can unlock the full potential of their employees and drive collective success.

These emerging theories and concepts reflect the evolving nature of organizational life in an increasingly complex and dynamic world. By embracing these new approaches, organizations can enhance their adaptability, foster innovation, and create more resilient and empowering environments. As we move forward, integrating these insights into organizational practices will be essential for navigating the challenges and opportunities of the future. Reflecting on these emerging theories, consider how they can be applied to enhance your organization's effectiveness and drive sustainable growth.

The Role of Technology, Blockchain, and AI in Organizations

Technology is transforming the landscape of organizations, fundamentally altering how businesses operate, compete, and interact with stakeholders. Among the most impactful advancements are blockchain and artificial intelligence (AI), which offer unprecedented opportunities for innovation, efficiency, and transparency. Understanding the role of these technologies is crucial for organizations aiming to thrive in the digital age.

Blockchain Technology

Blockchain is a decentralized ledger technology that provides secure, transparent, and immutable records of transactions. Its potential applications extend far beyond cryptocurrencies, impacting various aspects of organizational operations.

One significant role of blockchain in organizations is enhancing transparency and trust in transactions. By providing a tamper-proof record, blockchain ensures that all parties in a transaction have access to the same information, reducing the potential for fraud and errors. This is particularly valuable in supply chain management, where blockchain can track the provenance and journey of goods, ensuring authenticity and compliance. For example, companies like Walmart and IBM are using blockchain to improve food traceability, which helps quickly identify and address sources of contamination.

Blockchain also facilitates the use of smart contracts—self-executing contracts with the terms directly written into code. Smart contracts automatically enforce the terms of an agreement when predefined conditions are met, reducing the need for intermediaries and speeding up transactions. This can streamline processes in various sectors, including finance, real estate, and insurance. For instance, the real estate industry can benefit from faster and more secure property transactions, while the insurance sector can automate claims processing to improve efficiency and customer satisfaction.

In addition to enhancing transparency and efficiency, blockchain can also provide greater data security. Decentralization means that data is not stored in a single location, making it less vulnerable to hacking and data breaches. This is crucial for industries handling sensitive information, such as healthcare and finance, where blockchain can protect patient records and financial data.

Artificial Intelligence (AI)

AI encompasses a range of technologies that enable machines to perform tasks that typically require human intelligence, such as learning, reasoning, problem-solving, and decision-making. AI's impact on organizations is profound, driving innovation, efficiency, and competitive advantage.

One of the most prominent applications of AI in organizations is automation. AI-powered systems can automate repetitive and mundane tasks, freeing employees to focus on more strategic and creative activities. This improves productivity and reduces operational costs. For example, AI-driven robotic process automation (RPA) can handle tasks like data entry, invoice processing, and customer service queries, significantly speeding up workflows and reducing the potential for human error.

AI also enhances decision-making by providing advanced data analytics and predictive capabilities. Machine learning algorithms can analyze vast amounts of data to identify patterns, trends, and insights that would be impossible for humans to discern. This enables organizations to make data-driven decisions with greater accuracy and speed. For instance, in the financial sector, AI algorithms can predict market trends and customer behavior, enabling more effective investment strategies and personalized banking services.

Customer experience is another area where AI is making a significant impact. AI-powered chatbots and virtual assistants provide 24/7 customer support, handling queries and issues in real-time. These systems learn from interactions to continually improve their responses and provide more personalized service. Companies like Amazon and Netflix use AI to recommend products and content tailored to individual preferences, enhancing customer satisfaction and loyalty.

AI's role in innovation is also noteworthy. By enabling rapid prototyping and experimentation, AI helps organizations develop new products and services more quickly. For example, in the pharmaceutical industry, AI is used to accelerate drug discovery by analyzing biological data and predicting the efficacy of new compounds. In manufacturing, AI-driven predictive maintenance can foresee equipment failures before they occur, reducing downtime and extending the lifespan of machinery.

Integrating Technology into Organizational Practices

To fully leverage the potential of blockchain and AI, organizations must integrate these technologies into their core operations and strategies. This involves several key steps:

1. Developing a Clear Technology Strategy: Organizations need a well-defined strategy that aligns with their overall business

goals. This includes identifying specific use cases for blockchain and AI, setting clear objectives, and establishing metrics for success.

2. Investing in Talent and Skills: Implementing advanced technologies requires a workforce with the necessary skills and expertise. Organizations should invest in training and development programs to build a talent pool capable of managing and innovating with these technologies.

3. Fostering a Culture of Innovation: Encouraging experimentation and risk-taking is crucial for technological innovation. Organizations should create an environment where employees feel empowered to explore new ideas and approaches, supported by the necessary resources and leadership commitment.

4. Ensuring Ethical and Responsible Use: The deployment of AI and blockchain raises important ethical considerations, such as data privacy, bias, and accountability. Organizations must establish frameworks for ethical decision-making and ensure that their use of technology aligns with societal values and regulatory standards.

5. Collaborating with Technology Partners: Given the complexity of implementing blockchain and AI, organizations can benefit from partnerships with technology providers, startups, and academic institutions. These collaborations can provide access to cutting-edge expertise, tools, and platforms, accelerating the adoption and scaling of new technologies.

The integration of blockchain and AI into organizational practices is transforming the business landscape, offering new avenues for innovation, efficiency, and competitiveness. Blockchain's ability to enhance transparency, security, and trust, combined with AI's capabilities in automation, decision-making, and customer engagement, provides a powerful toolkit for organizations navigating the digital age. By developing clear strategies, investing in talent, fostering a culture of innovation, ensuring ethical use, and leveraging partnerships, organizations can harness the full potential of these technologies to drive sustainable growth and success. As technology continues to evolve, staying informed and adaptable will be key to maintaining a competitive edge and achieving long-term organizational objectives.

Sustainable and Ethical Organizational Practices

In an era where stakeholders increasingly demand accountability and responsibility, sustainable and ethical organizational practices have become essential for long-term success. These practices not only address environmental and social concerns but also enhance brand reputation, foster customer loyalty, and attract top talent. By integrating sustainability and ethics into their core strategies, organizations can create value for all stakeholders while contributing to a more equitable and sustainable future.

Sustainability in organizational practices involves adopting strategies and operations that meet the needs of the present without compromising the ability of future generations to meet their own needs. This encompasses environmental stewardship, social responsibility, and economic viability. Ethical practices refer to conducting business in a manner that is consistent with moral principles and values, ensuring fairness, transparency, and respect for all stakeholders.

Organizations are increasingly recognizing the importance of minimizing their environmental footprint. This involves reducing greenhouse gas emissions, conserving natural resources, and minimizing waste. Implementing energy-efficient processes and investing in renewable energy sources can significantly reduce an organization's carbon footprint. Tech companies like Google and Apple have committed to using 100% renewable energy for their operations, setting an example for others in the industry.

Sustainable supply chain management is another critical area where organizations can make a significant impact. Working with suppliers to ensure that materials and products are sourced sustainably involves using recycled materials, ensuring sustainable agricultural practices, and reducing transportation emissions. IKEA has committed to sourcing all its wood and paper products from sustainable sources, demonstrating a commitment to environmental responsibility.

Adopting practices that minimize waste generation and promote recycling can help reduce environmental impact. Companies like Unilever and Procter & Gamble have set ambitious goals to achieve zero waste to landfill in their manufacturing processes.

Social sustainability involves ensuring that business practices positively impact employees, communities, and society at large. Ensuring fair wages, safe working conditions, and respect for workers' rights throughout operations and supply chains are fundamental aspects of social responsibility. Patagonia and Fairphone are known for their commitment to ethical labor practices.

Businesses can contribute to the well-being of the communities in which they operate through philanthropy, volunteerism, and community development initiatives. Starbucks, for example, invests in community stores that support local economic development and job creation.

Promoting a diverse and inclusive workplace fosters innovation and reflects a commitment to social equity. Implementing diversity, equity, and inclusion (DEI) programs, ensuring equal opportunities for all employees, and actively addressing any forms of discrimination are essential practices. Companies like Microsoft and Salesforce are recognized for their strong DEI initiatives.

For sustainability to be truly effective, it must also be economically viable. Sustainable practices should contribute to the long-term profitability and competitiveness of the organization. Developing products that meet sustainability criteria can open new market opportunities and drive growth. Tesla's electric vehicles have positioned the company as a leader in sustainable transportation, attracting environmentally conscious consumers.

Adopting a long-term perspective in business planning helps ensure that investments in sustainability are aligned with future market trends and regulatory requirements. This reduces risks and enhances resilience. Companies like Nestlé and Danone have integrated sustainability into their long-term strategic planning.

Embracing circular economy principles, such as designing for durability, reuse, and recycling, can reduce costs and create new revenue streams. Philips, for instance, offers lighting products as a service, reducing waste and promoting resource efficiency.

Ethical business practices are foundational to building trust and maintaining a positive reputation. Organizations should be transparent about their operations, decision-making processes, and performance. This includes regular reporting on environmental, social, and governance (ESG) metrics. Transparency fosters trust with stakeholders and demonstrates accountability. Companies like Novo Nordisk and SAP are known for their comprehensive ESG reporting.

Adhering to legal and ethical standards in all business activities is essential. Organizations must implement robust compliance programs to prevent fraud, corruption, and other unethical behaviors. Johnson & Johnson, for example, has a strong compliance framework to ensure ethical conduct across its global operations.

Engaging with stakeholders, including employees, customers, investors, and communities, helps organizations understand their expectations and concerns. This engagement should be ongoing and include mechanisms for feedback and dialogue. Companies like Unilever and Coca-Cola have extensive stakeholder engagement programs to inform their sustainability strategies.

Several organizations exemplify sustainable and ethical practices. Unilever's Sustainable Living Plan aims to decouple growth from environmental impact and increase positive social impact. The company has committed to sourcing 100% of its agricultural raw materials sustainably and improving the health and well-being of more than a billion people by 2025. Unilever's focus on sustainability has enhanced its brand reputation and driven innovation across its product lines.

Patagonia is renowned for its environmental activism and commitment to sustainable practices. The company donates 1% of sales to environmental causes, uses recycled materials in its products, and advocates for policies that protect the planet. Patagonia's business model demonstrates that sustainability and profitability can go hand in hand.

Tesla's mission to accelerate the world's transition to sustainable energy has driven its innovation in electric vehicles and renewable energy solutions. By focusing on sustainability, Tesla has disrupted the automotive industry and established itself as a leader in sustainable transportation.

Integrating sustainable and ethical practices into organizational strategies is no longer optional; it is a business imperative. These practices not only address environmental and social challenges but also enhance competitiveness, drive innovation, and build trust with stakeholders. As organizations navigate the complexities of the modern business landscape, embracing sustainability and ethics will be crucial for long-term success and positive societal impact.

Reflecting on these principles, consider how your organization can further integrate sustainable and ethical practices into its operations and strategies. By committing to these values, organizations can contribute to a more sustainable and equitable future while achieving their business goals.

In this chapter, we explored the profound impact of sustainable and ethical practices on organizational success and the broader societal landscape. As the world grapples with environmental challenges, social inequities, and increasing demands for corporate accountability, organizations must embed sustainability and ethics into their core strategies.

We began by understanding the fundamental principles of sustainability and ethics, recognizing their importance in fostering long-term viability and trust. Environmental sustainability practices, such as reducing greenhouse gas emissions, conserving natural resources, and minimizing waste, are crucial for mitigating the impact of business operations on the planet. Organizations like Google, Apple, IKEA, Unilever, and Procter & Gamble exemplify how commitment to these practices can drive innovation and operational efficiency.

Social responsibility encompasses fair labor practices, community engagement, and diversity, equity, and inclusion (DEI). Companies such as Patagonia, Fairphone, Microsoft, and Salesforce demonstrate that ethical labor practices and inclusive work environments not only enhance organizational culture but also drive competitive advantage and societal impact.

Economic viability is essential for sustainability. Sustainable product innovation, long-term planning, and circular economy principles help organizations like Tesla, Nestlé, Danone, and Philips achieve profitability while adhering to sustainable practices. These companies show that economic success and sustainability are not mutually exclusive but rather mutually reinforcing.

Ethical business practices, including transparency, integrity, and stakeholder engagement, are foundational to building trust and maintaining a positive reputation. Organizations such as Novo Nordisk, SAP, Johnson & Johnson, Unilever, and Coca-Cola lead by example through comprehensive ESG reporting, robust compliance frameworks, and extensive stakeholder engagement programs.

The case studies of Unilever, Patagonia, and Tesla illustrate that integrating sustainable and ethical practices into organizational strategies is not just a moral imperative but a business necessity.

These companies demonstrate that sustainability and profitability can coexist, driving innovation, enhancing brand reputation, and creating long-term value for all stakeholders.

As we conclude this chapter, it is evident that embracing sustainable and ethical practices is crucial for organizations aiming to thrive in the modern business landscape. By committing to these values, organizations can address environmental and social challenges, enhance competitiveness, and build trust with stakeholders. Reflecting on these principles, consider how your organization can further integrate sustainability and ethics into its operations and strategies. By doing so, you can contribute to a more sustainable and equitable future while achieving your business goals.

In navigating the complexities of the contemporary business environment, staying informed and adaptable will be key to maintaining a competitive edge and achieving long-term organizational objectives. As organizations continue to evolve, the ability to integrate sustainability and ethical considerations into core business practices will remain a critical determinant of success and positive societal impact.

Conclusion

As we draw this exploration of organizational theory to a close, it's essential to reflect on the critical insights and practical strategies we've discussed throughout this book. Our journey has taken us from the foundational concepts of organizational structure and design to the contemporary challenges and future trends that shape the modern business environment. By synthesizing these insights, we can better understand how to lead and manage organizations effectively in a rapidly changing world.

The principles and practices covered in this book highlight the dynamic nature of organizations and the need for adaptability, innovation, and ethical leadership. From understanding the impact of globalization on organizational structures to leveraging advanced technologies like AI and blockchain, we have seen how external and internal factors necessitate continual evolution.

We have explored the importance of fostering a positive organizational culture and climate, the critical role of leadership, and the strategies for effective change management. We have also delved into the intricacies of decision-making, power dynamics, and the profound impact of sustainability and ethical practices on organizational success.

Reflecting on these themes, it is clear that the most successful organizations are those that are resilient, adaptable, and committed to continuous improvement. They are capable of navigating the complexities of the modern business landscape by fostering a culture of innovation, prioritizing sustainability, and maintaining a steadfast commitment to ethical practices.

In the following sections, we will revisit the key themes and lessons from this book, offering a synthesis of our journey and providing actionable insights for organizational leaders and practitioners. By embracing these principles and applying them thoughtfully, you can position your organization for sustained success and positive impact in the years to come.

Throughout this book, we have explored a wide array of concepts, theories, and practices essential for understanding and managing organizations effectively in the modern business landscape. At the heart of our discussion is the recognition that organizations are dynamic, complex systems that require continuous adaptation and innovation to thrive.

We began with the foundations of organizational theory, examining historical perspectives and core concepts such as rational, natural, and open systems. These frameworks help us understand the diverse ways organizations can be structured and managed. We also discussed the evolution of organizational thought, highlighting the shift from rigid, hierarchical models to more flexible, adaptive structures that emphasize collaboration and responsiveness.

Understanding organizational culture and climate is crucial for fostering environments where employees can thrive. A strong, positive culture aligned with organizational goals drives performance, while a supportive climate ensures that employees feel valued and engaged. Trust, at various levels within the organization, underpins effective relationships and is essential for innovation and resilience.

Leadership emerged as a pivotal theme, with a focus on both traditional and contemporary theories. Effective leaders are those who can inspire, support, and guide their organizations through change while fostering a collaborative and inclusive culture. We discussed the importance of aligning leadership practices with organizational strategy to drive success.

Innovation and change management are critical for maintaining competitiveness in a rapidly evolving market. We explored various models of innovation and the conditions necessary for fostering creativity and experimentation. Effective change management strategies, including clear communication, stakeholder engagement, and continuous improvement, are vital for navigating transitions and achieving desired outcomes.

Sustainability and ethical practices are increasingly important in today's business environment. Organizations must integrate environmental stewardship, social responsibility, and economic viability into their core strategies. This not only addresses societal demands but also enhances brand reputation and long-term success.

The impact of globalization, technology, AI, and blockchain on organizational structures and processes cannot be overstated. These forces are reshaping how organizations operate, compete, and interact with their stakeholders. Embracing these technologies and understanding their implications are essential for driving innovation and efficiency.

Throughout the book, practical examples and case studies have illustrated how these concepts and strategies are applied in real-world settings. Companies like Google, Apple, Patagonia, Unilever, and Tesla serve as exemplars of how commitment to innovation, sustainability, and ethical practices can lead to remarkable success and positive societal impact.

The most successful organizations are those that are adaptable, innovative, and committed to ethical and sustainable practices. By understanding and integrating the principles discussed in this book, leaders can position their organizations for sustained growth and impact. Reflecting on these insights and applying them thoughtfully will enable organizations to navigate the complexities of the modern business landscape and achieve long-term success.

Summary of Key Points and the Importance of Theory

Throughout this book, we have delved deeply into the foundational concepts, evolving theories, and practical applications that are critical for understanding and managing organizations in today's complex and dynamic business environment. The exploration of these topics has underscored the significance of organizational theory in providing a structured approach to navigating and addressing the multifaceted challenges that leaders and managers face.

At the core of our discussion is the recognition that organizations are dynamic, complex systems that require continuous adaptation and innovation to thrive. Organizational theory provides the necessary frameworks and tools to analyze and understand these complexities, enabling leaders to make informed decisions and implement effective strategies.

Foundations of Organizational Theory

Our journey began with an examination of the historical perspectives and core concepts of organizational theory. By understanding the evolution from early theories like Taylorism and Weber's bureaucracy to more contemporary approaches, we gain insights into how management practices have adapted to changing environmental conditions. These foundational theories offer essential frameworks for understanding the basic principles of organizational structure, behavior, and dynamics. They highlight the importance of efficiency, hierarchy, and formalization in achieving organizational goals.

Organizational Culture and Climate

A strong organizational culture and a positive climate are critical for fostering environments where employees can thrive. Culture encompasses the shared values, beliefs, and norms that shape behavior within the organization, while climate reflects employees' perceptions of their work environment. Together, they influence employee engagement, satisfaction, and performance. Theories on culture and climate provide leaders with tools to assess and shape these elements to align with organizational goals. A supportive culture and climate enhance innovation, collaboration, and resilience, enabling organizations to navigate challenges effectively.

Leadership and Management

Leadership is a pivotal theme, with both traditional and contemporary theories offering valuable insights. Effective leadership involves inspiring, supporting, and guiding the organization through change while fostering a collaborative and inclusive culture. Theories such as transformational leadership emphasize the importance of vision, motivation, and engagement, while servant leadership focuses on empowering and developing employees. Understanding these theories helps leaders adapt their styles to different contexts and challenges, ultimately driving organizational success.

Innovation and Change Management

Innovation and change management are critical for maintaining competitiveness in a rapidly evolving market. Innovation theories, such as those proposed by Amabile and Kanter, highlight the conditions necessary for fostering creativity and experimentation, such as autonomy, resources, and supportive leadership. Change management theories, including Kotter's 8-Step Process and Lewin's Change Management Model, provide structured approaches for implementing and sustaining change. These theories emphasize the importance of clear communication, stakeholder engagement, and continuous improvement in achieving successful change outcomes. By applying these frameworks, organizations can navigate transitions more effectively, reducing resistance and enhancing buy-in.

Sustainability and Ethical Practices

In today's business environment, sustainability and ethical practices are not optional but essential for long-term success. Integrating environmental stewardship, social responsibility, and economic viability into core strategies addresses societal demands and enhances brand reputation. Theories on corporate social responsibility (CSR) and stakeholder management offer frameworks for balancing profit with societal impact. Companies like Patagonia and Unilever exemplify how commitment to these principles drives innovation, customer loyalty, and operational efficiency. Understanding these theories helps organizations develop strategies that are not only profitable but also sustainable and ethical, ensuring long-term viability and trust with stakeholders.

Globalization and Technological Impact

The impact of globalization and technological advancements, particularly AI and blockchain, is profound. These forces are reshaping organizational structures, processes, and interactions with stakeholders. Globalization theories help organizations understand the complexities of operating in diverse markets, emphasizing the need for cultural sensitivity and local responsiveness. Technological advancements, such as AI and blockchain, offer new opportunities for efficiency, transparency, and innovation. Theories on technological adoption and diffusion provide frameworks for integrating these advancements into organizational practices. Embracing these technologies and understanding their implications are essential for driving innovation and maintaining a competitive edge in the global marketplace.

Practical Examples and Case Studies

Throughout the book, practical examples and case studies have illustrated how these concepts and strategies are applied in real-world settings. Companies like Google, Apple, Patagonia, Unilever, and Tesla serve as exemplars of how theory translates into practice. These organizations demonstrate the importance of commitment to innovation, sustainability, and ethical practices in achieving remarkable success and positive societal impact. By studying these examples, leaders can gain insights into best practices and strategies for applying theoretical concepts in their own organizations.

Importance of Theory

Organizational theory matters because it provides a structured approach to understanding complex organizational phenomena. Theories offer frameworks that guide analysis, decision-making, and strategic planning. They help leaders and managers identify underlying patterns, predict outcomes, and develop effective interventions. In a rapidly changing business environment, theory equips organizations with the tools to adapt and innovate, ensuring long-term success and resilience. By grounding their practices in robust theoretical frameworks, organizations can navigate uncertainties, capitalize on opportunities, and address challenges more effectively.

The exploration of organizational theory is not merely an academic exercise but a practical necessity for navigating the complexities of modern business. By integrating the insights and strategies discussed in this book, leaders can enhance their ability to drive organizational success, foster innovation, and create value for all stakeholders. Reflecting on these key points, consider how your organization can leverage these theories to achieve sustained growth and positive impact in an increasingly dynamic and interconnected world.

It's crucial to translate these theoretical insights into practical applications that can drive tangible results for business professionals. By applying these concepts in real-world settings, leaders and managers can enhance organizational effectiveness, foster innovation, and navigate the complexities of today's business environment. Here are key practical applications for business professionals, grounded in the theories and concepts discussed throughout this book.

Enhancing Organizational Culture and Climate

Creating a positive organizational culture and climate is fundamental for employee engagement and overall performance. Business professionals can start by conducting cultural assessments to understand the current state of their organization's culture. Tools like the Organizational Culture Assessment

Instrument (OCAI) can help identify dominant cultural attributes and areas for improvement.

Once the current culture is understood, professionals can work on aligning it with the organization's strategic goals. This might involve redefining core values, implementing recognition programs, and fostering open communication. Encouraging behaviors that reflect these values through leadership modeling and formal policies can reinforce the desired culture. A company aiming to foster innovation should encourage risk-taking and experimentation, provide autonomy to employees, and celebrate creative achievements. Regular town hall meetings, suggestion boxes, and feedback loops can help maintain a positive climate where employees feel heard and valued.

Implementing Effective Leadership Practices

Leadership significantly impacts organizational success. Business professionals should adopt leadership styles that align with their organizational context and goals. Transformational leadership, which involves inspiring and motivating employees towards a shared vision, can be particularly effective in dynamic environments.

Leaders should focus on developing strong relationships with their teams, providing regular feedback, and fostering an inclusive environment. Servant leadership, which emphasizes serving and empowering employees, can build trust and enhance team cohesion. By prioritizing the development and well-being of their employees, leaders can create a more engaged and productive workforce.

Practical steps include setting clear and inspiring goals, providing regular training and development opportunities, and maintaining open lines of communication. Leadership development programs can help managers enhance their skills and adapt to different leadership styles as needed.

Driving Innovation and Managing Change

Innovation is essential for staying competitive in today's fast-paced market. Business professionals can foster innovation by creating an environment that supports creativity. This involves providing resources, time, and space for employees to explore new ideas. Encouraging cross-functional collaboration and diverse teams can also spark creative solutions. To manage change effectively, professionals should apply structured change management frameworks like Kotter's 8-Step Process or Lewin's Change Management Model. These models emphasize the importance of creating a sense of urgency, building a coalition of support, and communicating a clear vision for change. Engaging employees throughout the change process, providing training, and celebrating short-term wins can help build momentum and ensure successful implementation. For instance, a company implementing a new technology can start by clearly communicating the benefits and necessity of the change. Involving employees in the planning process, offering comprehensive training programs, and recognizing early adopters can help reduce resistance and foster a smoother transition.

Integrating Sustainability and Ethical Practices

Sustainable and ethical practices are not only good for the planet and society but also enhance brand reputation and long-term viability. Business professionals should integrate sustainability into their core strategies by setting measurable goals for reducing environmental impact, such as lowering carbon emissions, minimizing waste, and sourcing materials sustainably.

Implementing ethical practices involves ensuring transparency, fairness, and accountability in all business operations. Regular ESG (environmental, social, and governance) reporting can demonstrate commitment to these principles and build trust with stakeholders.

Practical applications include adopting circular economy principles, such as designing products for durability and recyclability, and establishing robust compliance programs to prevent unethical behavior. Engaging with local communities through CSR initiatives can also enhance social impact and build positive relationships with stakeholders. For example, a fashion retailer can reduce its environmental footprint by using sustainable materials, implementing recycling programs, and ensuring fair labor practices in its supply chain. Communicating these efforts transparently to customers can enhance brand loyalty and attract environmentally conscious consumers.

Leveraging Technology: AI, Blockchain, and IoT

The integration of advanced technologies like AI, blockchain, and IoT can drive significant efficiencies and innovation. Business professionals should stay informed about the latest technological advancements and consider how they can be applied to their operations.

AI can be used to automate routine tasks, analyze large datasets for insights, and personalize customer experiences. For example, AI-driven chatbots can provide 24/7 customer support, while predictive analytics can optimize inventory management and enhance decision-making.

Blockchain technology can enhance transparency and security in transactions. It can be used to track supply chain activities, ensuring the authenticity of products and reducing fraud. Smart contracts can automate and enforce agreements, streamlining processes in industries such as real estate and finance.

IoT devices can improve operational efficiency by providing real-time data on equipment performance, environmental conditions, and supply chain logistics. For instance, IoT sensors in a manufacturing plant can monitor machinery health, predict maintenance needs, and reduce downtime.

Embracing Globalization

Globalization presents both opportunities and challenges. Business professionals should develop strategies that balance global integration with local responsiveness. Understanding cultural differences and adapting business practices to local markets are essential for success.

Practical applications include customizing products and marketing strategies to fit local preferences, building local partnerships, and investing in local talent. Companies should also ensure compliance with local regulations and standards. For example, a multinational company entering a new market can conduct extensive market research to understand local consumer behavior and preferences. Collaborating with local businesses and hiring local employees can provide valuable insights and enhance market entry strategies.

Applying organizational theory in practical settings enables business professionals to navigate complexities, foster innovation, and drive sustainable growth. By enhancing organizational culture, adopting effective leadership practices, driving innovation, integrating sustainability, leveraging technology, and embracing globalization, leaders can position their organizations for long-term success. Reflecting on these practical applications, consider how you can implement these strategies in your own organization to achieve your business goals and contribute positively to society.

We hope you have enjoyed our exploration of organizational theory and its practical applications, it's important to reflect on the journey we've undertaken and the insights gained. The dynamic nature of the business environment demands continuous learning and adaptability. By integrating the principles discussed in this book into your daily practices, you can navigate complexities, drive innovation, and build sustainable and ethical organizations.

One of the key takeaways from this book is the importance of understanding the foundational theories of organizational structure, culture, leadership, and change management. These theories provide the frameworks necessary for analyzing and improving organizational effectiveness. They help us understand why organizations behave the way they do and offer strategies for driving positive change.

Equally important is the need to stay abreast of emerging trends and technologies. As the business landscape evolves, so too must our approaches and strategies. Technologies like AI, blockchain, and IoT are not just buzzwords but powerful tools that can transform operations, enhance decision-making, and create new opportunities for growth. Understanding these technologies and their applications is essential for maintaining a competitive edge.

Sustainability and ethics are no longer optional but integral to modern business practices. Organizations that commit to sustainable practices and ethical behavior not only contribute to a better world but also enhance their reputation, attract loyal customers, and build a resilient business. By prioritizing environmental stewardship, social responsibility, and economic viability, you can create long-term value for all stakeholders.

Leadership plays a crucial role in navigating these changes. Effective leaders inspire, support, and guide their teams through transitions, fostering a culture of collaboration and innovation. By embracing diverse leadership styles and continuously developing your leadership skills, you can drive your organization toward success and resilience.

Continuous learning is the cornerstone of long-term success. The business world is ever-changing, and the ability to learn, unlearn, and relearn is crucial. This means staying curious, seeking out new knowledge, and being open to new ideas and perspectives. Engage with industry thought leaders, attend workshops and seminars, read widely, and encourage a culture of learning within your organization.

As you apply the insights from this book, remember that theory and practice go hand in hand. Use the frameworks and strategies discussed here as a guide, but also be prepared to adapt and innovate based on your unique circumstances and challenges. Reflect on your experiences, learn from your successes and setbacks, and continuously seek ways to improve.

The journey of mastering organizational theory and practice is ongoing. By committing to continuous learning and staying adaptable, you can navigate the complexities of the modern business landscape and achieve sustained success. Embrace the challenges and opportunities ahead with confidence, curiosity, and a commitment to excellence. Your efforts will not only drive your organization forward but also contribute to a more sustainable, ethical, and innovative business world.

www.ingramcontent.com/pod-product-compliance
Lightning Source LLC
Chambersburg PA
CBHW071158240526
45470CB00017B/337